A Girl's Guide to the Criminal Mind

A Girl's Guide to the Criminal Mind

THE SURVIVAL HANDBOOK

Alison Summers

Published by Kellow Press

www.alisonsummers.com

ISBN-13: 9781523902347

ISBN-10: 1523902345

Library of Congress Control Number: 2016907397

CreateSpace Independent Publishing Platform

North Charleston, South Carolina

Cover design by Herb Hernandez

Printed in the U.S.A.

For My Mother

Table of Contents

Preface

A few years ago, there was a popular series on the Biography Channel called *I Survived*. It consisted of dramatic testimonies by individuals who had escaped near-death situations. Sometimes the adversary was nature, and survivors told harrowing tales about being trapped by avalanches or shipwrecked in high seas. Men recounted those stories. Sometimes the accounts were of life-or-death struggles to fight off a vicious rapist or determined serial killer. These stories—equally heroic—belonged to the women.

The men who faced the wrath of nature knew the risks before they left home, and had taken appropriate precautions. They had trained before they took the helm of a boat or climbed a mountain. They had worn the appropriate protective gear. They attributed their survival to skill, instinct and training. In direct contrast, the survivors of violent sexual attacks were not prepared. The women said they didn't know what to do, that they never imagined they might face such a threat. Most of them said it was sheer luck they had survived.

Today, one in five women has been raped. The US Centers of Disease Control and Prevention estimate that 1.3 million American females annually experience a rape or attempted rape. Despite what the FBI describes as "an epidemic of sexual violence," it's more or less been left to the individual to figure out her own strategies for protecting herself. But how?

Following a study involving 108 rapists and 389 of their victims, forensic researchers at the Massachusetts Treatment Center for Sexually Dangerous Persons advised, "Knowledge might be the only weapon the victim has." It could literally be life saving. "Knowledge can provide a sense of power, as well as the confidence necessary to act rather than resign out of helplessness." That makes sense, doesn't it? Now where would a rape victim have obtained this vital knowledge?

She didn't get it at high school, that's for sure. Today, 10.5% of high school girls are victims of sexual assault. But though schools are mandated to hold fire and earthquake drills, and simulations involving a shooter roaming the halls, they're not required to hold drills on how to escape a rapist. Risk assessment classes aren't offered, nor is fighting back an important element in a girl's physical education curriculum. Cheerleading, yes. Self-defense, no.

Gavin de Becker is America's leading expert on predicting violent behavior. "By the time a girl has reached her teens," says de Becker, " she has gone from being an occasional sexual predatory prize to the leading sexual predatory prize. Accordingly, I don't think there's much information she needs to be protected from." However, the reluctance to address the topic continues at home. I've heard parents say they never discuss sexual violence because they don't want their teenage daughter to worry. Truly. I think finding oneself bound in the back of a van or facing a cold-eyed rapist would be much more worrying.

Will a young woman be offered this potentially life saving "knowledge" at college? Unlikely. Even though the threat to her safety increases drastically the moment she sets foot on campus— in 2015, the Association of American Universities reported that 27.2 percent of female students have been sexually assaulted—the best a freshman can usually hope for is a token self-defense class, and a rape whistle. And she probably won't get that.

"The vast majority of sexual assaults on campuses, in fact over 90 percent, are being perpetrated by serial offenders," says clinical psychologist David Lisak, who trains police and prosecutors about sex offenders. The same pattern has been found in towns and cities around the country. Whenever backlogs of rape-kits are processed and DNA identifications are made, the majority of rapists turn out to be repeat offenders. Roy Hazelwood, a legendary instructor at the FBI's Behavioral Science Unit at Quantico, Virginia, believes that "when you're dealing with rapes against strangers, I don't think there's a non-serial rapist. Some get caught before they become serial rapists."

Unless they're arrested, they don't stop after one rape. Why not? They're predators. It's in their nature to prey upon those who are weaker. And that's how rapists view women and girls. They expect us to be caught off-guard; they expect us to be frightened of them; they expect us to submit. We can't change their nature, but we can change our ability to deal with them.

In an FBI study of 41 serial rapists, Detective Ken Lanning asked one subject, "Barry, is there anything a woman could do to protect herself from someone like you? Are there any preventions she could take to lessen the chance of becoming one of your victims?" Barry Simonis (the Ski Mask Rapist) considered the question for a moment, and then shook his head. "Not really, no," he said, complacently. "If I really want a woman, there's nothing she can do to stop me."

But Simonis was wrong, as you're about to find out.

Introduction

"Being afraid of others is actually the fear that we are unprepared to protect ourselves."
—GAVIN DE BECKER

Thanks to traditional survival guides, hikers know to play dead when attacked by a bear, ranchers know where to apply a tourniquet to a rattlesnake bite, and surfers know it's best to punch a great white shark hard in the nose or eyes, and swim away fast. But the chapter that's always been missing is how to respond when attacked by a human predator. Since it is statistically more likely for a girl to be cornered by a rapist than to be mauled by a grizzly bear, I think the subject is worth at least a chapter in a survival guide. Actually it deserves more. Not just a chapter, but an entire book.

This is a survival guide for women and girls. It deals exclusively with human predators. On both counts, that makes it the first of its kind. Most people know more about four-legged predators than their own two-legged ones. It's hardly surprising. The information is more accessible. We can thumb through magazines like *National Geographic*, switch on documentaries on Netflix or Hulu, or tune in to TV channels like Animal Planet. But when the subject is human predators, there are no magazines with glossy photos, no Steve Irwins on camera to alert us to their habitats, and no David Attenboroughs to instruct us how they camouflage themselves to stalk their prey.

Inside these pages, you'll find everything you need to know about the human predator, and the best ways to protect yourself. You'll also gain insights from acclaimed experts in the field—such as behavioral profilers, sex crimes detectives, criminal psychologists, and forensic psychiatrists— into the way a predator typically thinks and plans his crimes. Where did they get their information? Straight from the horse's mouth.

"The perpetrators of crimes against women are interesting," Dr. Ken Magid explains, "because we have a chance through their interrogations and the testimony of others to examine what drives these predators to hunt and later hurt females. Then we have a few red flags of which to take notice." Of course, it's not only forensic psychologists and psychiatrists who could benefit from this information. If women knew those red flags, they would be in a better position to avoid these guys. You'll find out what those red flags are inside this book.

In 2013, a major scientific study proved that predator avoidance had influenced the brain size of certain prey animals in Africa and South America. "It was evolutionarily faster," according to the *Royal Society Journal's Biology Letters*, "for prey to alter its behavior than to evolve a swifter run."

The team's leader, Dr. Suzanne Schultz, explained that since changing behavior required a higher level of thinking, certain prey animals, such as monkeys, evolved a bigger brain. Once the large-brained animals became "capable of developing new strategies to escape attacks," the predators began hunting more "dim-witted" prey instead. Dr. Schultz sees a parallel with human beings: "When these findings are put into perspective, it makes sense that *being clever* should help individuals avoid or escape danger."

This is a book for women and girls interested in "developing new strategies to escape attacks" from sexual predators. While I can't guarantee the evolution of a bigger brain, as happened to those quick-thinking prey animals in Africa and South America, I am confident that the information has the potential to save lives. When a female freezes in a rape situation—as happens in over 50 percent of cases—it's because she doesn't know the best course of action to take. Detectives say it is common for the victim to say afterwards that she had never imagined people like the rapist existed and, unaware of other options, acquiesced. Nothing wrong with that: she survived, which is a victory in itself. The point is she was "unable to see other options." It's my goal to make you aware of what other options might be available to you.

Veteran FBI profiler John Douglas recalls the early days at the Behavioral Science Unit: "When you started profiling the cases, you could begin *seeing patterns*, and once you could start seeing patterns, you could start taking *proactive measures*." This book will outline those *patterns* so that you can choose your own *proactive* measures.

At the FBI headquarters in Quantico, Virginia, instructor Roy Hazelwood was renowned for his expertise on serial rapists. In one landmark study, Hazelwood interviewed forty-one offenders, collectively responsible for 837 sexual assaults and over 400 attempted rapes. Hazelwood was struck by their careful planning. "Their most common characteristic was patience." The rapists had kept abreast of the latest FBI investigative tools; they pre-meditated their crimes; they did not take unnecessary risks.

Hazelwood characterizes them as "highly organized." By learning how sexual criminals plan crimes, you'll be in a better position to assess risk and manage it. You can stay one step ahead of them by becoming "highly organized," too. Inside this survival manual, you'll find practical information such as what to keep in the trunk of your car, how to turn your closet into a makeshift panic room, how to make your home less attractive to a home invader, and the pros and cons of personal security devices like pepper spray, Mace, and the sound alarm.

You'll also find out how to 'fight dirty.' Learning how to break a rapist's nose, twist his testicles, gouge his eyes or crush his toes is hardly playing by the Marquis of Queensbury rules, but then rapists don't believe in the concept of a fair fight. They prefer to incapacitate their victims by slipping date-rape drugs into their drinks, hitting them over the head with tire-irons, or pressing chloroformed rags to their faces as they sleep. They prefer slim, petite females. As criminal profiler Pat Brown explains, "The tiny girl is easier to subdue, her body is easier to drag, her pants are easier to get off and she fits better in the trunk of his car." They're nothing if not practical.

Predators borrow techniques that worked for other predators. They like to follow the same playbook. When a girl is familiar with those strategies, predators lose their major advantage—surprise. Rapists rely heavily on surprise: climbing through a window when their victim is asleep, waiting behind trees for a passing jogger, or jumping out at a cyclist from behind a van.

Of course the best defense would be to never cross a predator's path. If only it was that easy. Most of us don't even know where that path is. Animals recognize predatory hunting grounds; when they stop at a watering hole, they remain alert. Not knowing where our predators hunt, we seldom proceed with the necessary caution. But you can find out the areas where predators gravitate in the chapter entitled *The Hunting Grounds*. And in *The Predator*, you'll learn how to adjust your level of security by taking a look around through predatory eyes.

Animals are able to identify their natural predators at first sight. It's not hard since they belong to a different species. But the human predator is an 'interspecies hunter,'— rare in nature— and he looks like us. Another problem is that unlike animal predators, which launch their attack with a roar, growl, snarl, or bellow, the human predator doesn't announce his violent intentions in advance. He is more likely to chat amiably as he lures his victim away from the crowd. However, there are telltale signs he's a predator in his appearance and the way he approaches a target. You can read about them in *A Wolf in Sheep's Clothing* and *An Actor Prepares*, as well as how to identify a predatory approach in *The Hunt*.

Predators study us before they approach. For too long that gave them an unfair advantage. It's time to level the playing field.

We're going to study them.

CHAPTER 1

The Investigation

*"The better women understand these processes
and issues, the better they will be able to recognize
these behaviors and combat them."*
— FBI CRIMINAL PROFILER JOHN DOUGLAS

et's start by reviewing the basic terms used by criminal profilers in an investigation. Some of them you may already be familiar with from TV shows like *Criminal Minds*, *NCIS*, *CSI*, and *Law & Order*.

UNSUB is an abbreviation for Unknown Subject.

MO refers to the modus operandi, or method of operation. MO covers the practical details of how, when, and where a crime is carried out, such as the time and place it occurs, the approach to the victim, the restraints and weapons used, and the types and level of injury inflicted on a victim.

The *signature* is a psychological profile of a crime scene. Investigators look at what the crime scenes reveal about the UNSUB's personality, motivation, and ways of expressing himself.

A *serial rapist* is a criminal who has committed three or more stranger rapes with a cooling-off period in between.

A *serial killer* is a criminal who has committed three or more stranger murders with a cooling-off period in between. The cooling-off period distinguishes him from a mass murderer or spree killer.

In this book, we'll be taking advantage of what FBI criminal profilers have learned through decades of interviewing serial killers. While your chances of encountering a serial killer are thankfully slim, the interviewers found that a serial killer has the same predatory mindset as a serial rapist. (And unfortunately, those encounters are not rare.) In fact, every serial killer had been a rapist until the day— accidentally or on purpose— he killed his first victim. Not only did the predator get a rush from taking a life, he realized he wouldn't have to worry about his victim going to the police. Murder had its practical side. And thus, a serial killer was born.

In investigating a sexual homicide, the police refer to the *three crime scenes*.

1. The first crime scene is where *the approach* by the UNSUB takes place.
2. The second crime scene is where the UNSUB *commits* the rape-murder.
3. The third crime scene is where the UNSUB *disposes* of the body and *removes* evidence.

By analyzing the evidence from the first crime scene, the police can decide whether the UNSUB is a *persuasion predator* or a *force predator*. A persuasion predator uses verbal means (the con) to lure a victim to the second crime scene. A force predator is less socially adept. His MO is to catch a victim by surprise with a display of brute force.

There are specific types of physical attacks:

A *blitz attack* is a sudden, extremely violent, and frenzied assault. Here, the predator uses excessive force or "overkill." Blitz attacks are reflected in multiple stab wounds, extensive cutting and mutilation, a high number of blows to the head and body, or multiple gunshots.

Sneak and stand is when a predator appears behind a victim, seemingly out of nowhere, to launch his attack.

Cold cocking is also known as *bop and drop*. As Pat Brown writes in her autobiography *The Profiler*, cold cocking is "any fast, violent maneuver that renders the victim unconscious or unable to fight." Ted Bundy relied heavily on cold cocking. Feigning injury, he would stand on crutches, waiting for the young woman carrying his briefcase to turn her back to him as she unlocked his car door. Then he would pick up a tire iron hidden behind a wheel, bludgeon his victim over the head, throw her unconscious body onto the passenger seat, and drive away.

Victimology is an important tool in crime analysis. Investigators try to figure out why a specific victim was selected. Asking these questions helps the investigator establish motive, which can lead directly to the perpetrator.

Homicide detectives also analyze whether a crime scene reflects a *disorganized* or *organized* offender. Special Agents Roy Hazelwood and John Douglas introduced these two categories to the FBI's Behavioral Science Unit at Quantico.

Disorganized and Organized Serial Killers

Many people assume that serial killers are insane, but insanity is a legal term, not a medical one. It refers to offenders who are so deluded that they don't know the difference between right and wrong. In fact, only five percent of serial killers are psychotic or schizophrenic. The other ninety five percent of serial killers—and 90 percent of serial rapists—aren't deluded. They're psychopaths. Professor Anthony Maden, chief clinician at the Dangerous and Severe Personality Unit at Broadmoor, England explains the basic difference. "Mental illness is where you have hallucinations and delusions. Mental illness comes and goes. It can get better with medication." However, a psychopathic personality "doesn't come and go. It's how the person is."

Schizophrenic serial killers really do hear voices commanding them to kill. BSU profilers refer to them as "disorganized" serial killers. They don't try to conceal their identity, and they are relatively easy to catch. Roger Depue, the first chief of the FBI's Behavioral Science Unit, explains that they "often don't leave the crime scene, they don't conceal evidence, they admit responsibility, and their crime scene will be strewn with clues." Psychopathic serial killers, on the other hand, are categorized as "organized."

"The organized killer—the true psychopath— is the most dangerous and intractable of all human predators," Depue states bluntly. "He prowls for his victims, in much the same way any cunning animal does." Thinking criminals are harder to capture. "These predators systematically stalk their victims, plan their actions, and carry out their crimes methodically, carefully disposing evidence linking them to the scene," says Depue. After his first homicide, one serial killer chastised himself— for his carelessness. "I made three fatal errors in the first twenty-four hours. I should have been busted." But Edmund Kemper says it was a learning curve: "I saw how loose I was and I tightened it up, and when it happened again and again, I got tighter and tighter, and there weren't any more slips."

Forensic psychologist Dr. Reid Meloy, author of *Violent Attachments*, emphasizes that serial predators are not reckless. "Predation is a purposeful,

3

planned, and emotionless mode of violence." When a prison psychiatrist questioned Ted Bundy about whether his rage at the crime scene was beyond his control—for example, could Bundy have stopped his violent behavior if a police officer appeared? — the serial killer seemed mystified by the question: "I wasn't totally oblivious to my survival." Of course he would have fled the cop. "I would equate that to a predator —having pulled down the prey— is approached by a bigger predator, and runs off."

In order to evade capture, the organized UNSUB spends a lot of time in the planning stages. As Edmund Kemper once explained to a detective, "Murder is very real. You have to do all the practical things of surviving." At trial he usually refuses an insanity plea. "Many of the murderers we interviewed were very sensitive to being called crazy or maniacal," recalls veteran BSU profiler Robert Ressler. (Ressler invented the term *serial killer*.) "They associated those characteristics with carrying out acts in ways that are stupid, foolish, and out of control."

When their plans succeed, serial killers see it as proof of their superior willpower and shrewd intelligence. They get a particular kick out of fooling investigators. Former FBI unit chief John Douglas, who interviewed more than 150 violent sexual offenders including Edmund Kemper, Richard Speck, and Gary Heidnik, comments: "It's all a game to the predator."

In the UNSUB's battle of wits, his real enemy is the police; the victim is the prize. Predators delight in duping law enforcement. In a letter dated October 1974, the BTK Strangler teased the local police chief in Wichita: "It's a big complicated game my friend 'the monster' plays. Putting victims number down, following them, checking up on them, waiting in the dark, waiting, waiting. Maybe you can stop him. I can't."

To cover his tracks, the organized predator familiarizes himself with the latest developments in forensic science and—in case he gets brought in for questioning one day—interrogation strategies. Some enroll in criminal justice courses, as Dennis Rader (BTK) did. They're fascinated by law enforcement. Over thirty years of interviewing serial killers, John Douglas found that "the main fantasy occupation was that of a police officer." Serial killers have even taken the police exam, but with a few exceptions—like David Gore, Mike DeBardeleben, and Gerard Schaefer— they failed the psych test.

Since retiring as an FBI instructor, Roy Hazelwood has been on the lecture circuit throughout the United States and Europe. During his time at Quantico,

Hazelwood collaborated with Dr. Park Dietz and profiler Janet Warren, on a highly regarded research project on sexual sadism. Thirty sexually sadistic rapists were selected for the prison interviews. Hazelwood reports being taken aback to find the participants were keen readers of books and articles by himself and others in his field. He quips that they "believed in the old axiom 'know thy enemy.'"

From death row, Gerard Schaefer actually volunteered for the study. "He wrote me that he tried to keep up with everything on homicide investigation," remembers Hazelwood. The serial killer was particularly struck by an article Hazelwood had recently published in the FBI's *Law Enforcement Bulletin*, and chatted to him as if they were professional colleagues. "My specialty as you may know," Schaefer added, "is Death Strap Bondage."

It wasn't unusual for serial killers to offer their expertise to BSU researchers. Ted Bundy was eager to be interviewed. "Dear Mr. Hagmaier, " he wrote in answer to one FBI profiler, "No problem. You're welcome if you want to drop by. I would certainly be interested in talking to you about the research being done by the BSU." Bundy also inserted himself into an active investigation. In 1986, Sheriff Dave Reichert, the head of the Green River Killer task force, received a letter from Ted Bundy who offered to help him develop a profile of the elusive serial killer. Bundy wrote: "Don't ask me why I believe I'm an expert in this area, just accept that I am, and we'll start from there." Dave Reichert, accompanied by Robert Keppel, flew from Seattle to interview Bundy in Florida State Prison.

CHAPTER 2

The Hunt

*"Put yourself in the position of the hunter.
That's what I have to do."*
— FBI PROFILER JOHN DOUGLAS

Serial killers refer to tracking victims as a "hunt." Ian Brady (The Moors Murderer) describes it as "an interesting and sometimes dangerous mode of recreation, like hunting." David Gore saw it as more challenging: "I hunted females like a big-game hunter hunts his prey." Unlike Gore, Robert Hansen actually was a big-game hunter. But Hansen wanted a bigger challenge than hunting moose and bears. He turned to releasing women in the Alaskan woods and shooting at them.

Forensic psychiatrist Dr. Art Norman, who examined Ted Bundy, testified to the judge that Bundy regarded murdering young women as morally "no different than shooting a deer and tying it to the hood of his car." Rather than feeling remorse, Bundy was proud of what he had done. "He'd gone after the game that was the most highly valued: attractive young women," says Norman.

The "hunt" has three distinct and consecutive parts—*trolling, stalking,* and *the capture.*

1. Trolling

Serial killers allude to the surveillance of possible victims as *trolling*. This is a fishing term used to describe the practice where a fisherman throws a net from a moving boat in a part of the ocean where he expects there to be an abundance of fish. A keen fisherman in his spare time, Edmund Kemper referred to his search for victims as "fishing expeditions," and the dead women as his "catch."

Trolling begins with a powerful urge. Michael Lee Lockhart describes how one morning, "I was in the shower washing up. And then it hit me. I had to go out and get me one." Forensic psychiatrists believe the impulse to kill is similar to the sudden craving that grabs hold of a drug addict. Ted Bundy talked of it as an irresistible force that struck suddenly: "I've got to go out *now* and start looking for something. " Apparently, this feeling was not unwelcome. Bundy remembers that he would hurry to the hunting ground in "a high degree of excitement, or arousal," to look for prey. Although "the feeling of sighting the animal would be different than shooting it," Bundy recalled, this stage of the hunt was just as "thrilling."

The organized serial killer doesn't take unnecessary risks or just "improvise." If he can't find a desirable target, he'll wait for hours until one appears, and if there are potential witnesses around, he'll come back later.

After the predator spots a possible target, he calculates how close he can get without being spotted by her or other people in the vicinity. Then he makes his move.

2. Stalking

At his trial, Dennis Rader told the judge there are three stages to a serial killer's hunt. Trolling was the first stage, he said, but then, "once you lock in on a certain person, that becomes stalking." During this second stage, the predator abandons his observation post and begins to follow his prey either on foot or in his vehicle. Profiler John Clarke describes the pursuit: "Like wild animals, psychopathic serial killers meticulously track their prey, watching their potential victim's every move, carefully planning the where and when of their attack." Predators don't impose a deadline on stalking. It can last for an hour, a day, often a lot longer. As Dennis Rader informed the judge, "Mrs. Otero and the girl, I stalked them maybe two or three weeks."

Stalking isn't merely the means to an end. Shadowing his prey—while maintaining his invisibility—makes the psychopath feel superior and powerful.

3. The Capture

As David Gore remembers, "My biggest rush was not the sex part, it was the capture. That was when I got a high." In nature, death follows immediately after the large predator pins down the smaller prey. "The predator will charge, lunge or pounce on the animal, slashing or biting the prey," says the *Royal Society Journal*. But a serial killer doesn't kill his prey for the same reasons animals do. It isn't about survival. He kills because it gives him pleasure. "You feel the last bit of breath leaving their bodies," Ted Bundy rhapsodized to FBI agent Bill Hagmaier. "You're looking into their eyes. A person in that situation is God."

The human predator is in no hurry to get the killing over. In fact, he prefers to prolong death by strangling his prey, rather than using a gun or a knife. Behavioral profiler Janet Warren recalls one subject confiding that he had breathed life back into a victim because she lost consciousness "too quickly." "I needed to see in her eyes that she knew I was going to take her life," the serial killer explained. It was the only way to "experience the power and control of being God-like."

Richard Ramirez, aka the Night Stalker, was of similar mind: "We've all got the power in our hands to kill, but most people are afraid to use it. The ones who aren't afraid control life itself." When it comes to that kind of hubris, there is no equivalent in the animal world.

Afterwards: Cleanup and Burial

"I took great pains in disposing of the women," David Gore claimed proudly. After the killing is over, the predator cleans up the last crime scene. He destroys any evidence and disposes of the victim's body. He chooses a trophy to take home so that the he can relive his crime. Gore explains, "It's like a deer hunter. He goes out and shoots this big buck with a nice rack of horns so he saws the horns off and brings them home to hang on his wall as a trophy. He wants to look at it and admire it. In the mind of the serial killer, we do the same, whether it's hair, jewelry, or whatever. We take it as a trophy from the kill, to admire."

Usually the trophy is a personal item such as a wallet, handbag, underwear, or a watch, but some serial killers prefer to keep photographs as mementos. "Viewing the pictures," Jeffrey Dahmer attested, "gave me a feeling of satisfaction that at least I had something to remember them by." Sometimes a killer gives a piece of the victim's jewelry to his wife or girlfriend so he can revel in the knowledge that his crime is on public display with no one being the wiser. A minority of serial killers —including Douglas Clark, Ted Bundy, Jeffrey Dahmer, and Edmund Kemper—cut off the victim's head. Since "I was the hunter," Kemper reasoned, "it was kind of an exulted, triumphant-type thing, like taking the head of a deer."

Collecting trophies isn't the smartest move, but the serial killer's pride triumphs over his instinct for preservation. The predator stashes his trophies away, despite the knowledge that this is evidence that could send him to death row one day.

CHAPTER 3

The Predator

*"Knowing what humans are really capable
of doing to each other makes you aware that civility
is a luxury which can be discarded at will."*
—HOWARD TETEN, THE FBI'S FIRST PROFILER

There is a popular saying in the field of forensic medicine: "Not all psychopaths are serial killers, but *all* serial killers are psychopaths." There is a similar saying about rapists. Not all psychopaths are rapists but, as FBI profiler John Douglas puts it, "All rapists would appear to be angry, aggressive psychopaths." In *The Psychopathic Mind*, the distinguished forensic psychologist Dr. J. Reid Meloy goes further: "Predatory violence appears to be quite *dependent* upon psychopathy."

Dr. Robert Hare invented the Psychopathy Checklist, the diagnostic tool employed in hospitals and prisons around the world. He says psychopaths *see themselves* as predators. "Psychopaths say there are predators and prey. When they say that, take it as factual. " And how does a non-psychopath prevent a psychopath from "preying" on her? Dr. Hare advises, "Your best defense is to understand the nature of the human predator." That's what we'll be doing in this chapter.

Ted Bundy admitted he had "a consciousness, which is comparable to a predator." When it came to rape or murder, the serial killer said, "There are not a lot of intellectual, moral, obvious considerations involved." There's a biological reason for Bundy's lack of remorse. With the advent of brain imaging, scientists discovered that a psychopath's brain has little to no activity in the area that governs empathy. There is also little to no activity in the area that regulates conscience. Psychopaths are genetically predisposed to ruthless behavior. As Dr. Martha Stout, author of *The Sociopath Next Door* observes, "If you take loving kindness out of the human brain, there's not much left except the will to win."

With a degree in psychology under his belt, Ted Bundy realized he was a psychopath. "I am in the enviable position of not having to deal with guilt," he acknowledged. He didn't see anything wrong with that. In fact, "I feel sorry for people who feel guilt."

Psychopaths are hard-wired to take advantage of others. These extreme narcissists regard society as a jungle where the strongest individuals—yes, that would be them—are *entitled* to destroy those who are weaker. In his journal, Dennis Rader (the BTK Strangler) depicts himself as a lone wolf: "The lone wolf stood at the top of the food chain. He took what he wanted, answered to no one, lived only for him, and killed whenever the urge hit him. Then he moved on. Nothing and nobody could stop a lone wolf."

Because of their inflated egos, serial killers are more likely to identify with the lion, king of the jungle, than a lone wolf. John Douglas—one of the early pioneers of criminal profiling— scorns the comparison. "Lions hunt for survival," Douglas points out. "They kill to feed themselves and their cubs." Serial killers, he says dismissively, "kill as a form of recreation." There are other significant differences. Lions do not hunt within their own species. Lions don't rape their prey before killing it. Lions don't enjoy making their prey suffer. A lethal bite or snap of the neck is where their hunt ends. And so on.

"The human predator is the greatest and most dangerous predator in existence," English serial killer Ian Brady once boasted. But serial killers and rapists aren't courageous, they're cowardly. Stalking involves a lot of furtive behavior like sneaking, peeping, and hiding. Nevertheless, it would be a mistake to underestimate the serial predator, because what he lacks in courage, he makes up for in cunning. He is also adept at blending into a crowd. "The killer knows the victim, but the victim doesn't know the killer," as Ted Bundy pointed out to Seattle homicide detective Robert Keppel.

However sexual psychopaths do share some peculiar characteristics. It's just a matter of being able to recognize them.

The Predatory Gaze

During his investigation into the disappearances of Denise Naslund and Janice Ott, Detective Keppel interviewed five girls who had rebuffed Ted Bundy's attempts to lure them away on the same afternoon. He recalls: "All the living witnesses from Lake Sammamish noticed that the 'Ted' who tried to pick them up had a strange stare while he was talking to them." Keppel remarks, "It was as if his eyes were transfixed on his prey."

It is often noted in medical journals and books that psychopaths have a weirdly intense stare. Psychologists refer to it as "the predatory gaze." The intensity of this stare, says Dr. Robert Hare, is "similar to the concentration with which a predator stalks its prey." For that reason, catching the eye of a psychopath can be unnerving. As one nurse confided to Dr. J. Reid Meloy about their psychopathic patient: "I felt as if he were staring right through me; when he looked at me, the hair stood up on my neck." Disturbed reactions to psychopaths are common among hospital staff, says Dr. Meloy, but this nurse's "comment is particularly telling because it captures the primitive, autonomic, and fearful response to a predator."

Dull Eyes

Predators have "dead eyes." There is no apparent life in them. Dr. Meloy continues, "It is my experience in forensic treatment to hear descriptions of certain patients' or inmates' eyes as cold, staring, harsh, empty, vacant, and absent of feeling." Other doctors have used the word *reptilian*. While Dr. Alexander Lowen agrees, "The eyes are dull; no light shines through them," he cautions, "This dullness of the eyes in no way reflects a dull mind. Quite the contrary."

An Emotional Robot

Dr. Helen Morrison interviewed serial killer Robert Berdella in prison. She was struck by the shallowness of Berdella's emotions. He talked "like a one-dimensional robot."

When he was a psychology undergraduate, Ted Bundy read *The Mask of Sanity* by Dr. Hervey Cleckley. It remains the most famous textbook on psychopathy of the twentieth century. "A psychopath," Dr. Cleckley wrote, "is in essence, an emotional robot, programmed by himself to reflect the responses that he has found society demands." Ted Bundy was quick to challenge this perception—"I am not a robot," he would volunteer during psychological assessments—but his defense lawyer Polly Nelson, who worked on Bundy's appeal, believed something vital was missing: "His natural instincts, I think, gave him no clue how a normal person would act."

Lacking empathy, psychopaths learn to fake it. While Bundy could be convincing, Dennis Rader seemed forced. He was terrible in social situations, according to former secretary Mary Capps, "He'd say, 'Hello, sir, how are ya?' but it was more robotic than sincere. He had this fake laugh . . . sort of like Jim Carrey when he'd go, 'Henh, henh. Henh.'" Mary remembers her boss as a "cold fish" and a "weirdo." He made her feel uncomfortable, she says. Even when he was being nice, her intuition signaled something was off. As she would learn later, her intuition was right.

CHAPTER 4

The Prey

"The best defense is plain ole common sense. Don't put yourself in a situation where you could be hurt."
—SERIAL KILLER DAVID GORE

n 1980, profiler John Douglas and FBI Special Agent Robert K. Ressler decided to interview serial killers to find out what made them tick. The information proved so useful that Roger Depue, the head of the Behavioral Science Unit, assigned other profilers to join the team. By the end of the decade, they had interviewed almost two hundred serial killers in jails around the country.

The profilers asked the offenders about their selection of victims. It came as no surprise to learn that young women were the favorite targets. It's the case today, too. Eighty-six percent of victims of sexual homicide are female. Most victims are between fifteen and twenty-eight years of age. It's a similar story with rape. Ninety percent of the victims are female; most are between fifteen and twenty-eight years of age. As John Douglas puts it, "The rape and murder of young women in our society is all too common."

The serial killers explained to FBI special agents that young women were "easy prey," because they "take too many risks." Ted Bundy even criticized his co-ed victims as irresponsible. "At that age you think you are invincible."

The predators said they had been attracted to young women who were "naïve and overly trusting." Pedro Alonso Lopez, who was responsible for the deaths of over three hundred girls in Peru, Ecuador, and Colombia, said he looked for girls who seemed gentle and innocent. "As head of the unit, I worked at maintaining my objectivity," Roger Depue wrote in a book about the early years of the Behavioral Science Unit. "But sometimes in my darker moments, it seemed to me that good humans beings were little more than unsuspecting prey."

The serial killers' most popular targets, in order of preference, were:

1. Females of high school or college age, including students, prostitutes, drug addicts and runaways
2. Children
3. Travelers of all ages
4. Women of all ages living alone

Did you see the last two? Yes, of *all* ages. It's a popular misconception that middle-aged and elderly women are safe from sex predators. In fact 8.3 percent of female victims of sexual homicide are in their forties, and 6.3 percent are in their fifties. After that there is a startling increase. The figures more than double! Fourteen percent of sexual homicide victims —almost one in seven — are women over the age of sixty.

"In profiling, our general rule of thumb is: the older the victim, the younger the offender," John Douglas explains. "With a victim in her seventies or eighties, we lower the initial age estimate into teen years." Teenage predators who lack their own vehicle usually hunt in their own neighborhoods. They target elderly women because they don't expect them to put up much of a fight.

The serial killers informed the FBI interviewers that they were quick to take advantage of "victims of opportunity." This category included hitchhikers, lovers at scenic lookouts, prostitutes, women who worked late at 24-hour businesses, and stranded female motorists. David Gore described his search as obsessive: "You get to a point where it literally consumes your life. I looked for potential victims wherever I went." It was lucky for him, said Gore, that "there are a lot of women out there who can't believe this could ever happen to them. I pretty much could get whoever I wanted."

Psychologists refer to this attitude as "the optimism bias." Dr. John Clarke says it stems from the belief that bad things only happen to other people. For example, "that other people are more likely to get skin cancer, have heart attacks, be mugged."

Case History: Debra Puglisi

Until she encountered Donald Flagg, "I was a classic cock-eyed optimist," says Debra Puglisi. Even at the age of forty-five, she had been "happiest to let my inner Pollyanna rule." Then one day Flagg broke into her home, murdered her husband, and abducted her. Debra was a prisoner in his home for five days. She was manacled, tied to a bedpost, beaten, and raped multiple times, before she managed to escape. Puglisi describes her life in the aftermath of the kidnapping: "That old way of being is gone. It was ripped away in minutes. The sweet ideals of trust, kindness, and openness—they were in the marrow of my bones—I loved them, defended them, and depended on them for more than forty years. Each and every day, I made decisions based on them. Now they seem comically simple and dangerously naïve."

The serial killers told BSU agents they were predisposed towards prostitutes because they were low risk: the women willingly got into a stranger's vehicle, and weren't likely to be reported missing for a couple of days. As Gary Ridgway, known as the Green River Killer, told detectives: "I chose prostitutes because I thought I could kill as many as I wanted, and no one would miss them." Drug addicts, homeless people, and teenage runaways were also deemed "low risk." Robert Berdella said of his victim Larry Pearson, a drug addict: "I quickly formed the opinion 'this is somebody that no one's going to end up missing.'"

The serial killers didn't feel at all guilty for taking lives. Detective Jim Byrnes asked Jerry Brudos: "Do you feel some remorse, Jerry? Do you feel sorry for your victims—for the girls who died?" Byrnes recalls, "There was a half piece of white paper on the table between us, and he picked it up, crumpled it in his fist, and threw the ball on the floor. 'That much,' he said. 'I care about those girls as much as I care about that piece of wadded-up paper.'"

The serial killers even blamed their victims for trusting them. Albert de Salvo expressed contempt for the college girls he molested under the pretext he was a scout for a modeling agency: "I hated them girls for being so stupid." The victims for whom the serial killers displayed the most scorn were hitchhikers. Despite acknowledging that the two eighteen-year-old girls he murdered "weren't much more than children," Edmund Kemper told detectives, "I felt that they were old enough to know better than to do the things they were doing, out there hitchhiking."

Woman's Intuition

Detectives say it's not unusual for a rape victim to tell them she had an uneasy feeling when her rapist first spoke to her, but since she couldn't rationalize it, she dismissed her initial impression. These days the police endorse intuition as a woman's first—and best —line of defense. Or as they describe it, "listening to your gut."

Intuition responds to pre-verbal signals faster than the conscious mind, which is why a victim can be confused about the source of her discomfort. Rather than search for meaning, she should make a quick exit according to security expert Gavin de Becker: "Would an animal in the wild that is suddenly overcome by fear spend any of its mental energy thinking, it's probably nothing?"

A day or two after escaping Ted Bundy at Lake Sammamish, the five survivors finally figured out what had bothered them about the handsome "injured" man. It had been different for everyone. Detective Robert Keppel took these notes.

"He was too intent."
"His eye contact was unnerving."
"He had looked uncomfortable."
"He spoke too fast."
"It sounded as if he rehearsed what he was saying beforehand."
"He seemed to have a hidden agenda."

Although none of the five women had known at the time what it was about Bundy that felt wrong, they heeded their intuition. Pat Brown, founder of the Sexual Homicide Exchange, says it can't be emphasized enough: "If a person or a situation feels wrong, walk away. Don't wait for further evidence."

If the stranger follows, tell him firmly but politely (these guys are thin-skinned) that you're not interested in talking further. Hold the eye contact so the guy realizes you have his number, and you are not easy prey.

CHAPTER 5

Following You

"I would find a girl walking."
—SERIAL KILLER GERALD STANO

Every woman knows it's risky to walk down an empty street at night. Should it be her problem alone? Not according to criminal profiler John Clarke: "Personal security, particularly for women, and particularly at night, should be a major priority for everyone." However, it's her problem by default when cities don't prioritize the safety of female residents by —for example—providing adequate lighting along suburban streets, or policing the exits of train stations after dark. And most of them don't. So, what will it take for a girl to get home safe? Here's what I suggest.

Just as there are classes you can take in defensive driving, there are strategies for defensive walking. The first step is to examine your route, and identify the places a predator could easily conceal himself. Look at dense shrubbery and poorly lit doorways. Large dumpsters also provide a lot of cover, as do trashcans in alleys. Change your walk so you can avoid those places.

Then there is the question of body language. Street toughness makes a predator think twice. He is looking for someone he can intimidate, so don't walk with your head bowed, or take small steps. Adopt a brisk stride. Hold your head high, and square your shoulders. Breathe from the abdomen and open your chest. Take up space confidently. Walk like a guy.

In nature, some animals evolved physical characteristics that made them an extremely unpalatable meal. Porcupines, for example, have incredibly sharp quills; that's why predatory animals avoid them. So, get prickly. For a woman, this means emphasizing that you are nobody's fool. Having an attitude.

What if you're passing a store, and the guy sitting outside says, "Hey, how are you doing?" If you ignore the greeting, it could be read as fear. Be sociable, but tough. Give him a brief and uninterested, "Hey, what's up?" Don't lower your eyes. Move on confidently, but let him know you're watching him. Human predators will generally avoid anyone who seems to be observing them shrewdly.

Predators on the street keep watch for distracted individuals. They zero in on girls absorbed by texting, or listening to an iPod. They creep up from behind in order to use the advantage of surprise. A target who appears keenly alert to what's going on around her is a turn off.

If you're walking along an empty street and you hear footsteps behind you—possibly a precursor to being cold-cocked—don't tentatively check over your shoulder. Turn your body completely around to face the person. Your body language should convey that you are not, as security expert Gavin de Becker phrases it, "a tentative, frightened victim-in-waiting."

If a man is coming toward you from the opposite direction, and you're getting a bad vibe, cross the road on a diagonal. Move confidently. Don't walk quickly or break into a run. From the middle of the road, look around to show you are keeping an eye on him. If he has vanished, reduce the chance of a "sneak and stand" assault by walking down the middle of the road.

What if you're walking down the street when a man appears beside you and demands money? Police recommend handing over the cash, but keep the transaction impersonal. Don't speak to the stranger or make eye contact. There is no guarantee he will lose interest in you once he has taken your wallet, so don't just hand it over, throw the wallet hard over his shoulder. While he is running to grab the wallet, you can take off in the opposite direction.

What's in Your Purse?

Despite the best-laid plans, you could find yourself walking down an empty, unfamiliar street or across a deserted parking lot at night. It happens to everyone. It is reassuring to know you can whip out one of the following items from your handbag.

1. A cell phone with 911 on speed dial so you won't lose precious seconds locating the keypad and punching the number in.
2. A personal security device like Mace, pepper spray, or a sound alarm. There are descriptions of how they work, and their pros and cons in the next chapter.
3. A Fenix flashlight like the police carry in TV crime shows. Since they come in many sizes, you will be able to find one that fits in your purse. The Fenix flashlight has a high-intensity beam. Not only does it illuminate dark corners brightly, but if you shine the light into the eyes of a pursuer, he will be temporarily blinded. This gives you time to run.

How to Use Your Fenix Flashlight

Have you seen how the police on TV use their flashlights? As you walk, clutch your Fenix with a firm grip. Hold the flashlight clenched inside your closed fist, so just the face is visible. Stride confidently along the street, using the flashlight to illuminate any dark areas where a predator might be concealed.

In the event a predator confronts you, react aggressively. Shout "911" loudly, or, "Get back." You want him to understand you are not easy prey. If he continues to approach menacingly, shine your flashlight directly in his eyes to blind him. This will disorient him, which buys you the time to do whatever comes next: such as reaching into your pocketbook to spray Mace or pepper spray in his eyes, or running while shouting, "Help! Call the police!" to alert others who might be in earshot. As you flee, make as much of a ruckus as you can.

Even if the assailant manages to wrestle the Fenix away, he can't hurt you with it like he could if you were holding a knife or gun. Flashlights are also convenient to take abroad. While Mace or pepper spray is illegal in some countries, no customs official is going to confiscate a flashlight.

Arriving Home

In Chicago, Tricia Pacaccio approached her front door keys in hand, but she never got to unlock it. She had been followed. Michael Gargiulo rushed to the porch, twisted Tricia's arm around her back, and in a blitz attack, stabbed her a dozen times.

When the streets are dark and empty, the goal is to get inside your home quickly. Take out the keys on approach to avoid fumbling in your handbag or checking for them in your pockets when you reach the door. Before you open it, look around to make sure no one is following you. If—a worst-case scenario—an assailant suddenly appears, you don't want him to be able to force you inside, so throw the house keys away, preferably into a neighbor's yard. As he runs for the keys, you run out into the street. Alternatively, if you are face to face with the offender, use those keys as a weapon. Stab him in the eye, then escape when he is too blinded to chase you.

If the light outside the front door is dim, obtain an LED light for your keychain or use the flashlight app on your cell phone to quickly illuminate the lock. (An LED light on a keychain is also handy for unlocking a car at night.) If there is no light switch just inside the door and you have to cross a dark hall to turn on the light, buy a night-light.

How Effective Are Martial Arts Classes?

There are good reasons to study martial arts but a quick course in fighting back is not one of them. Pat Brown—the nationally known criminal profiler—has an advanced degree in Tae Kwon Do. She confirms, "It would take a lot of training in the martial arts before they are of any use." And even an advanced degree in martial arts is no help to a victim who is bludgeoned from behind. Susan Rancourt didn't get to draw upon her black belt in karate when Ted Bundy cold-cocked her over the head with a tire iron.

If you're face to face with a predator, there is usually little time to find the right stance. David Kahn, a Krav Maga instructor, trains newbies to go straight for a rapist's eyes, gouging them with the thumb, and then following if necessary with a knee to the groin. There is an entire chapter coming up on how to do that.

How Effective Are Self-Defense Classes?

Self-defense classes are a great idea if they involve the "fighting dirty" tactics I'll describe later, because those moves buy you time to outrun an attacker. But be skeptical of claims that after one to three self-defense classes you'll be able to overwhelm an assailant. For one thing, the predator is likely to be bigger and heavier than you are. Edmund Kemper's victims—petite teenage girls—were confronted by a man who stood 6'6" and weighed in at three hundred pounds. Pat Brown believes it's irresponsible for instructors to make such promises. Students "feel it's safe to walk down a dark street or alley or into a deserted parking garage because they think they can actually beat people up after three hours of training. They can't."

Like all criminal profilers, Brown believes the most effective form of self-defense for women and girls is learning how "to think smart and keep from becoming a victim in the first place." Which is, of course, why you're reading this book.

Should You Carry a Weapon?

Mailmen carry citrus spray to ward off dog attacks. When you consider a woman is more at risk of being attacked by a rapist—there is one sexual assault every 1.9 minutes, according to the Department of Justice—than a mailman is of being mauled by a dog, it's remarkable that most of us don't carry *anything* for protection. Let's talk about what's available.

Most security experts agree that it's safer not to carry a deadly weapon. If an assailant gains control of a knife, for example, it is highly likely he will use it on you. If you carry a gun—unless you received the proper training—there is also a strong chance the attacker will gain control of it. However, there are many self-defense devices on the market now that are highly effective. They include Mace (although it is banned in some states), pepper spray, and personal alarms.

Since they are pretty inexpensive, you can experiment to find which gadget you prefer. Then, practice, practice, practice. The first time you use it shouldn't be facing a rapist. A canister of pepper spray might involve some fiddling until you figure out how to get the nozzle lined up. This would give an assailant enough time to grab you around the throat. Another disadvantage to using pepper spray is that if the wind is blowing in your direction, the pepper spray might get in your eyes. This is true of Mace as well.

A personal alarm is designed to frighten the attacker and alert other people to your plight. It's small enough to fit in a pocket of a coat. Since it comes with a cord, you can place it around your neck if you go jogging. Once you pull the pin, two loud sirens sound at different frequencies. If instead of fleeing, the attacker moves to grab the alarm, throw it away. While he runs to it, you can run in the opposite direction. Even if he picks it up, it's unlikely he would know how to turn off the alarm, which requires sliding the pin back into the alarm until it snaps into place. By then, you will be long gone.

If you notice you have been followed to the front door, pull the pin on your personal alarm. The extremely loud noise can wake neighbors and alert dogs to bark. The personal sound alarm requires a battery, so it's important to check regularly that it still works.

If you plan to go hiking in the wilderness, where you will be far from other people, a canister of Mace or pepper spray is probably more practical than a sound alarm.

Recommendations

1. Learn how to use the gadget that most appeals to you. It could be a flashlight, sound alarm, pepper spray, Mace, or a combination.
2. Practice the potentially lethal quick jabs outlined in the chapter called How to Fight Dirty until they become second nature.

CHAPTER 6
The Hunting Grounds

"Lacking the proper understanding of serial killers and how they operate, many people walk right into the predator's hands."
—CRIMINAL PROFILER PAT BROWN

Animals stay alert when they cross predatory hunting grounds. If they stop to drink water or rest, they listen for odd noises and scrutinize the undergrowth for movement. Human predators also have their favorite hunting grounds, but most of us cross them unaware. "The victim becomes a target because he or she is in a particular location staked out by the offender," states the FBI's *Crime Classification Manual*. Gary Ridgway (the Green River Killer) puts it more bluntly: "They were in the wrong place at the wrong time."

In this chapter, you will find out the most popular hunting grounds for human predators.

Secluded Areas

Criminal profilers assert that one of the riskiest things for women to do—after prostitution, hitchhiking, and taking drugs—is to be alone in an isolated scenic place, like a hiking trail or bike path.

Force predators hide in such unfrequented areas. They also like to troll the shores of lakes, dams, and rivers. David Gore cruised the Florida coastline. "Secluded beaches became one of my favorite hunting grounds.

I would simply drive up and down, pulling into these secluded beaches, and if I saw a car parked there, I would step up the beach and see if it was a woman by herself."

Woods and mountains are appealing territory, too. Force predators stalk lone hikers, bird watchers and cross-country skiers. A force predator—lacking in charm and verbal acuity—depends on brute strength, and in an isolated area, he can assault his victim on the spot without having to lure her away first. Profiler Pat Brown, a fitness enthusiast herself, lives by this rule: "Heading to secluded areas alone—even on a mountain bike (which can be knocked down)—is basically a bad idea, any time of day."

If you're going to the woods or mountains, select a well-populated path and stay with the crowd, or invite one of your friends to come along. If none of them are into the great outdoors, consider joining a group like Meetup or the Sierra Club so you can co-coordinate your favorite fitness activity with other nature lovers.

Case History: The Bike Path Rapist

Altemio Sanchez lived just outside of Buffalo. The Bike Path Rapist, as Sanchez was dubbed by the press, knew the local scenic areas like the back of his hand. Posing as a jogger, Sanchez's MO was to find a secluded location, clear away foliage, and lay out strips of tape, which he intended to place across his victim's mouth to prevent her from screaming and alerting others.

Sanchez murdered three women and raped at least fourteen—local detectives believe the true figure is probably double that—along exercise paths, wooded short-cuts, and bike paths in western New York State over a fourteen-year period.

Isolated railroad tracks are another favorite hangout for predators. Angel Maturino Resendiz, known as the Railroad Killer, committed almost all his murders beside train tracks. By using the railroad system, the transient killer was able to jump on and off trains in three countries, eluding homicide detectives in the United States, Canada, and his native Mexico for many years.

In Salem, Oregon, serial killer Jerry Brudos grabbed fifteen-year-old Liane Brumley as she walked to school along the Southern Pacific Railroad tracks. The girl pretended to believe him when—gun in hand—he promised she wouldn't get hurt if she came quietly. Liane allowed Brudos to lead her the long distance toward his car, but upon spotting a woman in her garden, the girl broke free and ran screaming to her for help. Having lost his victim, Brudos fled the scene.

Suburban Streets and Local Parks

Sexual assaults in large city parks are so common that only the most sensational cases make the newspapers. Trees and bushes provide cover, allowing the predator to stalk his target unseen. Dense foliage also means a predator can assault his victim without fear of interruption. In 2012, one such predator, David Albert Mitchell, raped a seventy-three-year-old woman who had been bird watching in a wooded area near the Strawberry Fields section of New York's Central Park.

Case History: Chandra Levy

In 2001, residents of Washington, DC, were mystified by the disappearance of a twenty-four-year old congressional intern who had gone running in Rock Creek Park. When family members revealed the young woman was having a secret affair with Gary Condit, a married congressman, a nationwide media frenzy ensued.

Extensive searches failed to locate Chandra Levy. More than a year after she disappeared, a man walking his dog found human remains in a remote area of the park. Chandra had been raped, and tied to a tree. According to the coroner, she died from exposure.

In 2010, a serial rapist, Ingmar Guandique, was convicted of her murder. Several years before, Guandique had pleaded guilty to raping two women in Rock Creek Park around the time Chandra went missing. (Those assaults had failed to garner much press attention.) The prosecution's case relied heavily on the testimony of fellow prisoner Armando Morales, who said Guandique had told him he had killed the young intern. Guandique denied this conversation had ever taken place.

Guandique's lawyers appealed. In 2016, prosecutors dropped the case, admitting they had withheld evidence that would have cast doubt over their main witness's credibility.

Chandra Levy's murder remains unsolved.

Police advise women who like to jog in city parks to:

1. Avoid the secluded and remote parts of the park.
2. Avoid times when there aren't many people around.

Pat Brown says she goes to the park at midday when there are so many other runners, it's as safe as running with "fifteen of your closest friends." Women who run along suburban streets should avoid times when there aren't people around. "Dusk or dawn is a prime time for serial killers to target joggers," Brown continues. "There are few people out at that time on the paths and streets, and the killer does not have to worry about witnesses."

Bus Stops
The predator watches as a bus discharges its passengers. If he spots a desirable target, he follows her.

Sometimes the predator boarded the bus at an earlier stop. From his seat, he observes his fellow passengers closely. He decides on his prey. When she gets off the bus, he does, too.

Case History: The Scarborough Rapist
Paul Bernardo trolled bus stops in Toronto. When a young woman got off the bus alone, the serial rapist—soon to become a serial killer—would follow her along the dark streets of his Scarborough neighborhood. Once she drew near an area of dense foliage, he would break into a run, overwhelm the woman with a blitz attack, and drag her into the undergrowth, where he would rape her at knifepoint. Known to police only as the "Scarborough Rapist," Paul Bernardo is believed to be responsible for raping at least sixteen women there. After he moved to the city of St. Catharines with his bride Karla Homolka, the couple raped, tortured, and murdered three teenage girls.

Parking Garages
If you're crossing a deserted parking garage, it's always best to appear vigilant. According to serial killer David Gore, "I could sit in any parking lot and watch

and observe women, and I could tell you how alert they were." He gives this advice: "Know who's around you! Look at the cars parked around your car! Is there anyone sitting in them? If so, just keep your eye on them."

Seven percent of stranger rapes—an alarmingly high figure— occur inside parking garages. Often in stairwells. Parking garages are also a common site for abductions. It takes only minutes for a predator, hiding behind a vehicle, to cold-cock a passerby, bundle her body into his trunk, and drive away.

The FBI refers to the van as "the sex offender's vehicle of choice," and recommends women give vans a wide berth. Avoid walking beside vans, and don't park beside one. Candice DeLong, a former FBI spokesperson on the issue of women's safety, explains: "Serial killers attack their victims by pulling them into their vans while the women are trying to get into their cars from the drivers' seats."

Since predators are anxious to avoid security cameras, the best place to park is in full view of one. The worst parking spot is next to a wall, because your car could be boxed in by another vehicle. If you return to your car to find there is a man in the next vehicle—just sitting there idly—don't automatically pull out your keys. You could come back later when he has gone, or if that's not an option, get into your car from the side farthest away. Another possibility is to ask a police officer to accompany you back to the car. Cops respect gut feelings. Most of them will oblige if you tell them that the stranger makes you uneasy.

On the other hand, asking a security guard for help is risky. This job provides a gun and it doesn't require a criminal background check. Criminal profiler Pat Brown explains why she wouldn't do it: "Did you know that a serial killer's number-one most likely job is security guard?"

Before you climb into your vehicle, check the backseat. (Remember how in TV crime shows, the killer suddenly pops up from behind, and grabs the driver in a ligature hold?) Instead of checking your cell phone for messages, the FBI advises that you quickly "Lock the doors and drive away."

Public Spaces

Persuasion predators are attracted to heavily populated places because there is more prey to choose from, and a predator is less likely to stand out in a crowd. "Serial killers don't just strike in dark alleys or secluded streets," David Gore liked to remind people.

Thirty-one percent of serial killers troll for victims in public places such as malls, bus stations, amusements parks, bookstores, arcades, campuses, and taverns. "It's the anonymity factor," Ted Bundy explains. "First of all, if you're among strangers, you're less likely to remember them. Secondly, you're conditioned almost not to be afraid to deal with strangers."

Malls

Since malls are such a popular destination for teenage girls, it's no surprise that sexual predators flock there, too. Jerry Brudos abducted nineteen-year-old Linda Salee from outside a department store in the Lloyd Center, in Portland. Brudos flashed what looked like a police badge and told Linda he was arresting her on suspicion of shoplifting. Ted Bundy approached eighteen-year-old Carol Da Ronch as she browsed in Waldenbooks at a Utah shopping mall. He identified himself as "Officer Roseland."

Christopher Wilder, a wealthy Florida businessman, looked every inch the fashion photographer he claimed to be. He drove a Ferrari and he carried some impressive camera equipment. During his eight-month killing spree, Christopher Wilder abducted girls from malls in Oklahoma City, Tallahassee, Merritt Island, Las Vegas, and Merrillville, Indiana.

Wilder's MO was to approach a teenage girl in a mall and introduce himself as a fashion photographer. To establish his credentials, Wilder would produce a *Vogue* magazine cover and claim it as his work. He would tell the girl that she had the specific "look" he was after for his newest assignment, and suggest they go outside into the natural light where he could take some test rolls. Once they emerged from the mall into the parking lot, he would viciously attack the girl, throw her into his vehicle, and drive away.

Gas Stations

Gas stations are another popular site. Police advise women drivers to take a really good look around before getting out to pump gas. If you see a suspicious-looking man or group of men lurking nearby, you should drive to the next gas station.

When it's time to pay for gas, always lock the vehicle and take the keys with you. After getting back in the vehicle, head straight for the highway.

Schools

Michael Lee Lockhart used to park outside middle schools at the end of the school day. Once he had chosen his victim, he would follow her as she walked home.

Ted Bundy's preferred hunting ground was university campuses. "College girls are such beautiful people," he enthused. Nevertheless, on several occasions he surveilled grade schools, too. He abducted twelve-year-old Lynette Culver in front of Alameda Junior High School in Pocatello, Idaho, and grabbed twelve-year-old Kimberley Leach outside her middle school in Lake City, Florida.

Bundy didn't always stay outside school gates. One evening, Bundy sidled into a high school auditorium in Bountiful, Utah, just as the curtain went up on a drama club production. He chose a seat behind seventeen-year-old Debra Kent and her parents. At intermission, Bundy followed Debra outside. She headed for her vehicle, intending to pick up her younger brother from the nearby rollerblading rink. Bundy cold-cocked Debra, threw her unconscious body into his Volkswagen, and drove away.

Case History: Ted Bundy and Georgann Hawkins

On college campuses, Ted Bundy's customary ruse was to feign injury and ask for help carrying books or a briefcase to his car. From death row, Bundy described one such abduction—that of Georgann Hawkins—to the Seattle detective who headed the investigation into her death. Bundy told Robert Keppel that he had parked his VW in a shadowy tree-lined area at the University of Washington. He knew the campus well, and he headed toward the lane between the girls' dormitories. "I was handling a briefcase and some crutches." Feigning difficulty, he asked several female students to carry his briefcase to his car, but it was late at night, and each of the girls turned him down. Then he encountered Georgann Hawkins: "I was moving up the alley. About halfway down the block I encountered her. I asked her to help me." The kind-hearted Georgann Hawkins readily agreed to carry the briefcase for the man on crutches.

As they arrived at his VW, Bundy asked the girl to open the passenger door. Once Georgann turned her back, Bundy grabbed a crowbar that was hidden behind one of the tires. "I knocked her unconscious with the crowbar. I put her in the passenger side of the car and drove away."

Bars and Clubs

Persuasion predators feel right at home in bars. They often don't bother with a ruse. They try to seduce their victims instead. Ted Bundy described himself "chattering, flattering, and entertaining" girls he targeted at Dante's Tavern in Seattle. Serial killer Arthur Shawcross charmed potential victims in the Borderline Bar and Grill in Poughkeepsie, New York: "No one in that bar ever had a clue of what a sick, twisted fucker I really was." Shawcross believed he was able to convince them he was a really nice guy, because "I acted like I wanted to get to know them."

So what is likely to catch a predator's eye? Two things. A woman who is alone. A woman who is drinking. As Ted Bundy put it, "The more she drank, the more she would lend herself to stereotypes." Yes, it's the old-fashioned double standard. Sex predators are quick to judge women for drinking; they are also critical of women who wear revealing clothing. "Sex offenders don't think like normal men," as FBI profiler Candice de Long points out, so they are "always on the alert for what they perceive as 'provocative' behavior."

Jeffrey Dahmer used to comb the gay bars in downtown Milwaukee. He introduced himself to young men as a photographer, and offered a generous fee for a quick photo shoot. Serial killer Glen E. Rogers also did his trolling in bars, as did Robert Browne. Sometimes Browne didn't even try to get the victim to a second crime scene. Having persuaded Melody Bush to leave the bar with him, once they were outside "I used ether on her. Put her out. And then I used an ice pick on her."

Ted Bundy professed to be astonished that a young woman would go home with a stranger: "I read an article recently. It was by a woman. Millions of gullible women are reading this. It says, 'my biggest thrill is to go to a bar and pick up somebody I don't know and take them home with me.'" While most women wouldn't leave a bar with a man they had just met, detectives recommend they should be cautious about meeting up later, too. There have been cases where a serial killer or rapist asked for a woman's phone number, then attacked her as soon as they were alone on their first "date." Until you know him better, dates should be in public places.

With the easy availability of date-rape drugs, clubs have become extremely popular hunting grounds. The crowds are big, which means it is easy for the predator to blend in. There is usually no bartender keeping an eye on him, so it's easy to spike a drink.

There's also little risk, as a predator sees it. No one is likely to intervene if he pulls a semiconscious woman out the door. The other patrons and the bouncers will assume he is taking his very drunk girlfriend home. New York City detectives believe that is how the disappearance of twenty-five-year-old Laura Gaza unfolded in December 2008.

Security footage shows Laura leaving Marquee, a trendy Chelsea club, with a man she just met on the dance floor. This was uncharacteristic behavior according to her friends. Michael Mele, a registered sex offender, drove Laura to his home in upstate New York, where he suffocated her, then dumped her body in a wooded area near Scranton.

Recommendations for Clubs

Okay, they're a predator's playground, but it's fun to go dancing. So, just don't go alone. Profiler Pat Brown recommends that you "resort to the ancestral behavior of traveling in packs." That means when you're dancing, don't lose sight of your girlfriends. Stay close. Take turns on the dance floor so there is always someone to watch over the drinks. Or, even better, finish your drink before you get up to dance. If you want to go to the ladies room, and there's no one to watch your drink, take it with you.

Some predators save themselves the price of admission, and troll the exteriors of clubs. So if you go outside to smoke or talk on your cell phone, stay close to the front door.

If you don't want to cross a dark, empty parking lot to get to your vehicle —smart thinking! —take a cab or an Uber home instead, or phone a friend to pick you up in their car. You can collect your vehicle the next day.

Wining and Dining

Do you enjoy dropping by your neighborhood bar for a glass of wine and a cheese plate? As any bartender can tell you, the predatory guys usually come in after eleven. So think about going earlier, if you don't want a lounge lizard grabbing the stool next to yours.

If you're there when it's late, and a guy offers to buy you a drink, the safest move is to distance yourself politely. Why be polite? Because if he's a predator, he has a lot of rage. If you're rude he might follow you when you leave the bar, intent on teaching "that bitch a lesson."

What if you politely turned him down, but he won't go away? He protests, "But I'm not dangerous!" (Funny thing: it's always dangerous men who insist they're not dangerous.) Discounting your refusal is a red flag. Tell him loudly and emphatically to leave you alone.

By drawing the attention of bar staff and other patrons to the exchange, you have deprived him of his invisibility At that point, he will likely push his stool back and walk away. But if he persists in making the moves on you, or if he just sits there glaring at you, ask the bartender or manager to intervene.

When you're ready to leave, don't walk to your car by yourself. Ask the bartender for the number of a cab company, or call a friend to pick you up.

Date-Rape Drugs

Poisonous snakes and deadly spiders direct their venom glands at their prey to paralyze them so they won't be able to fend off an attack. Date-rape drugs like Rohypnol and GHB serve the same purpose for human predators.

Date-rape drugs are illegal, but they're easily bought on the Internet. These drugs are a predator's dream come true. They're fast acting and, unless a victim receives quick medical attention, hard to trace in the bloodstream. Though ubiquitous now, they've been around for a long time. David Gore boasted that he and his cousin Fred Waterfield were using date-rape drugs in the 1980s, "before people knew about it. You had to be real selective on how you used it, but it did work great."

The most widely used date-rape drug is Rohypnol. These pills are commonly known by their street name, "roofies." Rohypnol is a prescription sedative produced by Hoffmann-La Roche. It is both tasteless and odorless. The drug dissolves quickly in liquid and the victim starts to experience its effects within twenty minutes. Rohypnol pills are small and white, with a line across one side and the word *Roche* stamped on the other, with the number one or two in a circle.

The next most prolific date-rape drug is GHB, known on the street as Easy Lay, Liquid Dream, Scoop Her, and Get Her to Bed. A pharmaceutical company does not make GHB. It's produced in illegal drug labs or private homes. GHB is a clear liquid that resembles water. It takes effect in ten to fifteen minutes. Often, after ingesting Rohypnol or GHB, victims are left with no memory of what happened to them.

Predators have always experimented with ways to render their victims unconscious. Louisiana serial killer Robert Browne—who confessed to forty-eight murders—walked his suburban streets late at night with a chloroform-soaked rag in a plastic bag. He knew the residences where women lived alone, and he would go from one to the next, trying doorknobs. When he found an unlocked door, he would make his way to the bedroom, press his saturated rag to the sleeper's face and rape the unconscious woman.

John Wayne Gacy's victims—slim, attractive young men and teenage boys— were guaranteed to be in better shape than the overweight, middle-aged serial killer, so he also relied on chloroform to subdue them. In 1978, twenty-seven-year-old Jeffrey Ringall was walking through New Town, an area of Chicago crowded with bars and discos, when Gacy approached him. After a friendly chat, the older man invited him to smoke a joint in his car. While Ringall was taking a puff, Gacy forced a chloroform-soaked cloth to Ringall's face until he passed out. When the captive came to, he was in Gacy's house, and he had been handcuffed. Overnight, Ringall was drugged repeatedly and raped several times. He woke up the next morning, lying underneath a statue in Chicago's Lincoln Park, fully dressed.

Serial killer Jeffrey Dahmer also relied on drugs. His MO was to offer his guest a refreshment, then spike the drink with Lorazepam, an anti-anxiety medication. Robert Berdella added sleeping pills to Larry Pearson's drink, then injected him with an animal tranquillizer. His intention was to put the victim in a zombie-like state. For Berdella, Gacy, and Dahmer, drugs were an effective way to control strong young men, but they were also experimenting for the thrill of it. "I simply wanted to see what happened," Berdella told his psychiatrist.

Although most predators dissolve the drug in drinks, it can also be injected into food. Christopher Wilder had booked a model for a photo shoot, and when she arrived, he offered her pizza. She consumed a couple of slices while Wilder fiddled with the lights. Once the model became comatose, he raped her.

Doctors say they have been seeing more of this specific "paraphilia" or sexual deviation involving an assailant forcing sex upon a comatose victim. The rest of us have become more aware of it too, now that America's favorite "Dad"

Bill Cosby stands accused of drugging dozens of women and sexually assaulting them once they were unconscious. But Cosby is not the first celebrity to be accused of this crime, as you'll find out in a later chapter.

CHAPTER 7

A Wolf In Sheep's Clothing

"He wanted me to see him as he liked to think of himself: sophisticated, urbane, polite, respectful. All his movements and conversation were designed to show that he was not a monster, despite all documentary evidence to the contrary."

—TED BUNDY'S LAWYER

When trolling for victims, a sexual criminal has to camouflage "his predatory nature," the English serial killer Ian Brady writes, so he can "move freely among the herd without being detected."

To lure his victim away, the predator strikes up a conversation. This is a low risk strategy because if he is rebuffed, the predator can just walk away: no crime has been committed. It's also low risk because he is flying under the radar. No one looks twice at two people having a chat. When the "approach" works, the victim accompanies him voluntarily to the next crime scene; no one sees her go, or who took her.

"The first goal of a serial killer," David Gore told an interviewer, "is to get his or her intended victim to drop their guard and be caught unaware." For that to happen, the predator has to win his victim's trust. Unfortunately, persuasion predators are rather adept at winning people's trust. Crime writer Ann Rule was once Ted Bundy's partner at a Seattle crisis hotline center. She describes him as "one of those rare people who listen with full attention, who evince a genuine caring by their very stance."

Persuasion predators try to convey sincerity. "If you have a psychopathic personality," remarks Dr. James Hicks, "you are a smooth talker, and you intuitively recognize how to approach people in order to charm them, or gain their sympathy." It is not unusual for a woman a serial killer failed to lure away to admit later: "I almost went with him. He was *so nice.*" Survivor Janice Graham remembers Bundy like this: "He was polite at all times. Very sincere. Easy to talk to. He was real friendly and he had a nice smile." Dr. Helen Morrison describes the eighty plus serial killers she examined as belonging to "a murderous fraternity that is full of charmers."

Tricking their prey isn't just a means to an end. Forensic psychiatrists say that "duping delight" is common to all psychopaths. "The first thrill is the deception," admitted serial killer Arthur Shawcross, while Michael Lee Lockhart—who preyed on girls age fourteen to sixteen—boasted, "I could pretty much pick anyone off the street, and they would follow me anywhere like a puppy dog. It was that easy."

A typical approach by a persuasion predator unfolds like this:

1.   A stranger turns up out of the blue.
2.   He asks you for assistance.
3.   The assistance will involve being alone with him.

Are there any other clues that could identify a persuasion predator? Yes. There are a few as it happens.

In a Manner of Speaking

He's likely to talk too much. Just like used-car salesmen, persuasion predators have a gift of the gab. And just like used-car salesmen, they can push too hard. A reporter who interviewed the Canadian serial killer Clifford Olson recounts: "He talked fast, staccato. He jumped from topic to topic. He sounded glib, slick."

John Wayne Gacy described himself as a "motormouth." Dr. Helen Morrison, who interviewed Gacy several times, agrees: "The clinical name for such a condition is *logorrhea*, one of the symptoms seen in persons who are in a manic state. They talk on and on, even if they're not hyperactive, and they can't seem to stop."

Energy Disturbances

Psychopaths tend to have a kinetic energy. When a psychopath fixes his intense gaze on you, Dr. Ken Magid explains, it can feel like he "cast an almost irresistible, hypnotic spell, which draws you toward the psychopath." Some recipients find the kinetic energy exciting; others find it disturbing. For some, it's both.

Serial killers are often described as charismatic. Charisma is different from charm. Hitler was utterly charismatic, but no one says he was charming. Whereas the relaxed charm of a George Clooney springs from a genuine liking for other people, psychopaths feel contempt for others, so their attempts to charm can seem forced. John Wayne Gacy, for example, came across as fake and ingratiating. Unfortunately, it wasn't the case with Ted Bundy. "Ted could charm any woman in the bar," his cousin Alan recalled.

How do you guard against a charming predator like Bundy? Replace the adjective "charming" with the verb "to charm." Assess the stranger: "Is this guy trying *to charm* me?" If he's a persuasion predator, that's exactly what he's doing.

Persuasion Strategies

To lure his victim away, the predator invents a ruse. The ruse usually requires immediate action, because like any high-pressure salesman, the predator doesn't want his target to have time to "think it over."

The most common ruses are:

1. Pretending to be lost and asking for directions.
2. Asking for assistance with a physical task, such as carrying a heavy object, or starting a stalled car.
3. Needing help with an emergency such as finding a missing child or pet.

These behaviors are unusual in themselves. Why? Because when it comes to asking for directions, well…normal men are notorious for not asking for directions, and today with the advent of cell-phones and GPS, they're even less likely to ask a woman how to reach their destination.

A stranger who requests help with a physical task is behaving atypically, too. As one criminal profiler points out, "Normal men are not going to ask a woman they are barely acquainted with for help with a menial job. They will choose a man their own age or older."

Requesting your help with an emergency? Once again, normal men head straight for another man first. The FBI recommends this reply: "I think you'd be better off asking a man." Normal men respect the fact that women need to be suspicious of approaches by male strangers.

The Pity Play

Dr. Stanton Samenow, who spent thirty years studying sexual criminals at St. Elizabeth's Hospital for the Criminally Insane in D.C., says that to a psychopath, "kindness is weakness." Kindness doesn't earn any gratitude. "If he were kind to others, he would be seen as a sucker. And that is how he perceives those who are kind to him."

Predators design ruses that will exploit a victim's kindness. "The good are defenseless," Caryl Chessman, the Red Light Rapist, wrote in his prison memoir. "I'm sorry to say it like that but it's true. It's because they're good. " The ruses often involve a play for the target's pity.

No serial killer has ever known how to exploit pity better than Ted Bundy. Struggling with crutches, his arm in a sling, or his leg in a cast, Ted Bundy would approach a young woman and ask her to help with a task. It usually involved carrying something to the "injured" man's car, like library books, skiing boots, or a briefcase.

At Lake Sammamish, Bundy lured his victim with a fictitious sailboat. One arm in a sling, Bundy approached twenty-three-year-old Janice Ott as she lay sunbathing. The kind-hearted girl accompanied him to the parking lot to help him lift his sailboat onto the roof rack of his vehicle. At his daughter's memorial service, Mr. Ott told the crowd, "She had a burning desire to help. It doesn't surprise me a bit that she would agree to help someone in need."

Is it too risky these days to be a Good Samaritan? No. The problem wasn't that Janice helped an injured man. The problem was she left the safety of a crowded beach with him. To protect yourself from persuasion predators, Gavin de Becker, the country's leading expert in predicting violent behavior, recommends keeping two words uppermost in your mind: Privacy and Control (or PC, for short.) "Privacy is defined here as isolation or concealment," says de Becker. "Control exists when one person is persuaded or compelled to be directed by the other."

In other words, as long as she stayed on the beach chatting to him, Janice Ott was in no danger from the serial killer. It's only when a predator "gets Privacy and Control, he can victimize someone," says de Becker. " If he does not have PC, he is not dangerous, period."

Camouflage

In nature, predators evolved camouflage. *The Journal for the Royal Society* in Britain explains, "The colors of its fur or feathers, as well as its patterns and markings, help the animal to blend in with its surroundings." Human predators also camouflage their predatory nature—not only when they're hunting, but in every aspect of their daily existence.

On the night before his execution, Ted Bundy finally confessed to his mother that he was a serial killer. He told Louise Bundy over the phone that although the son she loved did exist, there was a different Ted she didn't know about. To be successful as predators, serial killers and serial rapists have to dupe their families, friends, co-workers, and communities as to their true nature. David Gore marvels: "People could not believe someone like me was committing such horrible crimes. I did not act or look like a serial killer."

Before he goes trolling a predator chooses clothes that will help him blend in. Even though Gerald Stano took pride in being fashionable—"I'm no slouch when it comes to clothes"— he wore nondescript clothing when he went on a hunt. The style of clothing for these expeditions is usually conservative. Ted Bundy was attired for tennis—white t-shirt, white shorts, and white tennis shoes— when he strolled along the shore at Lake Sammamish. He could have come straight from a nearby country club.

The FBI's *Crime Classification Manual* informs detectives that a serial rapist or killer "typically will be dressed neatly, either in business or casual attire." Dennis Rader's neighbors said that even on weekends he was well dressed, with carefully pressed shirts and pants, and highly polished shoes.

When it comes to looks, predators have to work with what nature gave them. On screen, serial killers tend to be handsome men. But in real life for every Michael Lee Lockhart, there is an ugly guy like one-eyed, snaggle-toothed Henry Lee Lucas; for every Ted Bundy there is a weaselly Gary Ridgway; for every Richard Ramirez, there is a Jerry Brudos, a hulking giant with a bad case of acne.

The majority of serial killers, however, are just ordinary looking guys. When they walk away from crime scenes, people don't give them a second glance. Dr. Helen Morrison reports that most serial killers—she has interviewed over eighty of them— are "average men who are overweight and doughy." Roger Depue, former head of the FBI's Behavioral Science Unit, says "One thing that never ceased to amaze me was the way so many of these killers appeared normal."

CHAPTER 8

An Actor Prepares

"He may strike up a conversation as a prelude to the attack. He may impersonate a role such as a police officer or security guard to gain the victim's confidence."
THE FBI'S CRIME CLASSIFICATION MANUAL

The Internet has made it easy to purchase phony security passes, ID cards, authentic-looking uniforms, hard hats, badges, and other paraphernalia associated with a specific job or workplace. "Predators come in many forms and guises," attests John Douglas who founded the FBI's Investigative Support Unit. "They're all dangerous." Here are some of the most popular occupations—real and phony—for sex predators.

Fake Occupations

The Police Officer

"When I approached a woman as a cop" says former deputy sheriff David Gore, "they just assumed they were safe, because I was a cop." In recent years there has been a steep climb in the number of predators using fake cop uniforms, police badges, and IDs. Many of the badges and IDs look so real that police say even they find it difficult at first glance to tell the difference.

Today the "number-one ruse is to pose as a cop," says Robert Keppel. "It happens all the time." A former homicide detective, Keppel investigated more than fifty serial killers including Ted Bundy, who impersonated a police officer several times. When he approached Carol Da Ronch in a Utah mall, he identified himself as Officer Roseland. The Oregon serial killer Jerry Brudos also tried to pass himself off as a cop. Brudos's ruse was to catch up with a girl leaving the mall and "arrest" her on suspicion of shoplifting. "I had a badge, looked just like a real police badge," Brudos recalls. "I bought it right there, in Lloyd Center; it was a toy, but you'd have to look real close to be sure." The serial killer also purchased a pistol. It, too "was a toy, but it looked real."

Fake cops are so common now that police departments have set up special units to catch them. Lieutenant Daniel Villanueva heads the Miami Dade Police Impersonator Unit. Since the unit was established in 2007, it has investigated more than eighty phony cops. "It's definitely a trend," says Villanueva.

Alarmingly, some serial killers actually have been police officers. David Gore was an auxiliary sheriff in Florida. He says the job provided invaluable training for a serial killer: "I learned how crimes were investigated, what cops look for, etc. And I honed my skills to a science." Gerard Schaefer was a police officer in Martin County, Florida, when he ordered Mary Alice Briscolina and Elsie Lina Farmer into his police cruiser. Schaefer told the girls they were under arrest. They were never seen alive again.

Scenario

A police officer orders you to accompany him to the station. If you haven't committed any crime, should you refuse? Tell him that first you'll need to verify his identity with 911. As David Gore remarks: "A real cop will not have a problem with this." If he doesn't appear fazed when you call 911, ask him to hand you his ID. Start reading the details to the operator. If he flees at that point, leaving you with his bogus ID, so much the better because his fingerprints will be all over it.

While David Gore's ID was actually genuine, he acknowledges that a call to 911 would not have been in his best interests. "If someone would have told me that, I would have got away as quickly as possible," he states emphatically.

The Firefighter

On Halloween night in 2005, Peter Braunstein disguised himself as a firefighter. Braunstein entered an apartment building on Twenty-Third Street in Manhattan. Braunstein went straight to the apartment of a former work colleague. He ignited two homemade smoke bombs and pounded on the door, demanding access. Upon seeing his firefighter uniform and smelling the smoke, she allowed him into her apartment. Then her twelve-hour rape and torture ordeal began.

In most cases, predators don't go to the theatrical extremes that Braunstein—an Off-Off-Broadway playwright—did by lighting smoke bombs. Usually, they just rely on a fake firefighter uniform and a ruse. "Ted told me one time he went to this high school and pretended to be a firefighter, with a badge and all," remembers David Gore, who became friends with Ted Bundy in prison. "He spotted this girl who was a cheerleader and went up to her and told her that her house had caught fire and her parents had sent him to come and pick her up and bring her home. And she went with him."

The Real-Estate Client

In Great Barrington, Massachusetts, serial rapist Mike DeBardeleben posed as a newly arrived businessman looking for a home for his wife and himself. He made an appointment with Terry McDonald to see a house at some distance from town. Terry was later found dead in the basement. DeBardeleben had strangled her with her panty hose.

Veteran profiler Roy Hazelwood comments: "The real-estate women are available, accessible. To me, it is the most dangerous legitimate profession in America. They go with total strangers to isolated areas on weekends, nights, and holidays. I think that's the reason DeBardeleben chose them as victims. He could get them away. Generally, no one was suspicious if they were gone a considerable amount of time."

"Mom was just a very unsuspecting, very trusting person," Terry's daughter Lynn remembers. "She always looked for the good in people. She was always positive about them." These days, many real estate firms won't send an unaccompanied female realtor to show an isolated property to a male client.

Case History: Kosoul Chanthakoummane

In 2007, Kosoul Chanthakoummane was found guilty of the murder of Sarah Walker, a top-selling realtor for DR Horton in McKinney, Texas. The killer had made an appointment for an hour earlier to look at an empty house with a different realtor. But after talking on the phone with Chanthakoummane, the realtor had a funny feeling about him, and she asked her husband to accompany her.

When Chanthakoummane saw the realtor's car pull up, he was perturbed to see she had brought a man with her. The killer decided to abort the plan. Without identifying himself, he walked past the house. However, as he turned the corner, he saw an Open House sign and he walked inside the home to investigate. He found Sarah Walker waiting in the kitchen. In a frenzy, he stabbed the realtor twenty-seven times and then fled.

The Delivery Guy

Most of us don't think twice about opening the door to a mailman, UPS guy, or deliveryman, but these identities are easy to fake. UPS uniforms, for example, can be bought at Goodwill stores. The police advise that you should never open your door to a delivery guy unless you have been expecting him.

Real-Life Occupations

The Security Guard

Though most security guards aren't serial rapists, an awful lot of them are. Even more alarming, it's also the most common job for serial killers. The advantage for someone with a history of sexual assault is that most employers don't do a criminal background check. The job is also attractive to predators who wanted to be cops but failed the psych exam. The uniform bestows the authority they fantasize about. It also comes with a company-issued gun.

Although the pay isn't great, turnover is high, and there are always openings somewhere. Malls and stores need security guards; so do businesses, hospitals, parking lots, and office buildings.

The Bouncer

This is another profession where a lot of employers don't check applicants' criminal backgrounds. It also gives predators access to sexily dressed young women—some of them in a state of inebriation.

Darryl Littlejohn was an ex-con with a rap sheet that included six felony convictions, one of which was for armed robbery. However, none of those arrests precluded him from being employed as a bouncer at the popular Manhattan bar where he abducted Imette St. Guillen.

Case History: Imette St. Guillen

Imette St. Guillen, a twenty-three-year-old student at John Jay College in Manhattan, was studying for a Master of Arts in Criminal Justice. One Friday night Imette and her best friend Claire went out drinking to Pioneer, a popular bar in Tribeca. At three a.m., they left the bar. Claire hailed a cab, but Imette insisted they try another bar called The Falls. They argued. "I stood there," Claire tearfully told a jury, "and I watched her walk away." Claire headed home.

Imette St. Guillen dropped by The Falls for one last drink. At closing time, the bouncer, Darryl Littlejohn, walked the semi-conscious woman outside through a side door, and then he pushed her into his car. Seventeen hours after Imette had left the bar, police discovered her dead body wrapped in a filthy blanket beside a desolate, weed-choked area off the Belt Parkway in Brooklyn. Traces of the date rape drug GHB were found in her system.

The Repairman

This is the third most popular job for serial killers. Why? "A yellow hard hat opens a lot of doors for you," Dennis Rader explains.

The job provides a convincing reason to enter a woman's home. Albert DeSalvo, known as The Boston Strangler, was a professional handyman who targeted older women living alone. DeSalvo would turn up at their doors, claiming he was sent by the management to repaint or fix a potential problem.

If a repairman unexpectedly shows up at your door, it's advisable-—even if you have seen him doing maintenance work around your building—to tell him it's an inconvenient time. After he departs, call the management to verify they sent him.

Cary Stayner was employed at a motel just outside Yosemite, California. In 1999, Stayner murdered forty-two-year-old Carole Sund, her fifteen-year-old daughter, and the daughter's friend, Silvina Pelosso. He had gained access to their room by knocking on the door and telling Carole Sund he had been sent to fix a leak.

A lot of hotels and motels hire handymen without doing a criminal background check. So, if a man arrives at your hotel door unexpectedly, and claims he has been sent to check the air-conditioning, heating or TV, tell him you will call the front desk first to ask what they're concerned about. If the front desk confirms they sent him, you can schedule the visit for a time you're not in the room. Also, guests are not obliged to let anyone into their room to check the minibar, so you have the option to tell reception that the minibar may only be inspected in your absence.

The Truck Driver

More than twenty-five long-haul truck drivers sit in federal prisons, convicted of being serial killers. They include Keith Hunter Jesperson (the Happy Face Killer), Wayne Adam Ford, Robert Ben Rhoades, Scott William Cox, Dellmus Colvin, and Bruce Mendenhall.

In recent years, more than five hundred bodies of missing women have been discovered near major highways. FBI investigators believe that serial killers operating across several states are responsible for the majority of the victims. Many of the victims were prostitutes who were last seen at truck stops or gas stations. Other victims included hitchhikers, women whose cars had broken down, and women with jobs at businesses along major highways.

For restless serial killers, the freedom and anonymity of the road is attractive. A long haul trucker only needs to converse with the strangers at loading docks, weighing stations, twenty-four-hour businesses and truck stops. Those people probably won't remember him. The serial killer's truck is a mobile crime scene. He can commit the crime in the back, and then dump the body near the highway. By the time the body is found, the killer can be hundreds, perhaps thousands, of miles away.

The Highway Serial Killings Initiative

Between 1980 and 2009, the bodies of more than 500 missing women were discovered near major highways across the country. Some bodies had been dumped in quiet rest areas, others at busy truck stops, and some had been tossed like garbage along the road. On April 6, 2009, in response to what it called a "crisis" situation, the FBI announced the Highway Serial Killings Initiative, wherein law enforcement in different states would begin comprehensively sharing and analyzing computer data on their highway killings.

Similarities in MO and signature led FBI investigators to believe that serial killers operating across several states were responsible for most of the dead bodies. Gradually, their suspicions fell on long-haul truck drivers. Two hundred suspects, most of them truck drivers—some of whom had prior records of sexual assault—have so far been identified by the Highway Serial Killings Initiative as persons of interest in the highway serial killings, but to date only ten suspects have been arrested.

Though the known number of women killed and dumped near highways is already astonishingly high, the FBI believes the true number of missing women has been "grossly underreported," and that a more accurate total is likely to be in the thousands.

The Photographer

A significant number of serial killers have been professional photographers (Wayne Williams, William Bradford, and Rodney Alcala to name a few). There are even more serial killers who were amateur photographers (Christopher Wilder, Jeffrey Dahmer, Murray Glatman, and others).

The appeal for sex predators is obvious: a photographer has complete privacy and control over his subject. Sometimes the rapist behind the lens is a fashion photographer. It's been alleged that New York City photographer Terry Richardson sexually harassed dozens of his models. Film director Roman Polanski raped thirteen-year-old Samantha Geimer during a photo shoot for *Vogue* magazine.

Serial killer Murray Glatman advertised for models to pose for photos he claimed were for a detective magazine. In the 1950s, detective magazines were notorious for lurid covers featuring scantily clad women, their wrists bound, cowering before a man with a knife. In the Behavioral Science Unit, profilers referred to them as "rape and murder manuals," remembers Roy Hazelwood. Glatman's pretense that he was a photographer for a detective magazine provided him with an excuse to handcuff the model, or bind her with a ligature, thus placing her under his control.

Celebrities

Bill Cosby is just the latest TV celebrity to be accused of multiple sexual assaults. Jimmy Savile, the British TV star, abused hundreds of children and teenagers. Between 2001 and 2007, Anand Jon, who was a familiar face on television's *America's Next Top Model*, enticed teenage girls and young women to his Los Angeles studio by promising them modeling work. Today Anand Jon is behind bars, convicted of multiple rapes.

There was also a serial killer who made regular TV appearances. In 1978 Rodney Alcala seemed quite the catch on *The Dating Game*: a handsome, talented photographer, who had graduated from the UCLA School of Fine Arts. He had a brilliant mind as well, with an IQ of 160. Rodney Alcala won *The Dating Game*, but his victory was short-lived. After shaking hands with him, bachelorette Cheryl Bradshaw changed her mind about going on a first date with Alcala. His energy was "creepy," she told the producers. Her intuition proved to be correct. Before moving to California, Alcala had committed two murders in New York City. After his arrival on the West Coast, he killed two more women. He didn't stop after *The Dating Game*.

Rodney Alcala is now behind bars. Although he was found guilty of ten rape-murders, homicide investigators suspect the figure will surpass fifty. He has become known as The Dating Game Killer.

Props

Predators often employ props to win their victims' trust. Some props are used to convey professionalism—fake badges, IDs, uniforms, hard hats—while others are designed to create the impression of harmlessness. Ted Bundy studied prop making during a semester in the theater department of Temple University. He was proficient at making arm and leg casts out of plaster of Paris. In April 1974, after Susan Rancourt's disappearance at Central Washington University, 110 miles southeast of Seattle, two co-eds contacted detectives. Their stories were virtually identical. They had been approached as they exited the library by a man wearing an arm sling. He asked for help carrying his books to a brown VW.

"I asked him how he hurt his arm. He told me it was a skiing accident. He had hit a tree," one of the statements read. "When he looked at me, it sort of bugged me—two big eyes staring at me weirdly. I remember that the passenger seat wasn't in the car. When we were standing next to the car, he started complaining about his arm: 'oh my arm hurts.' He opened the door and told me to start the car. I dropped the books, turned around and ran back to my apartment."

Some serial killers try to create the impression of being loving fathers by scattering toys on the backseat of their vehicle, or installing a child safety seat. Some serial killers produce photos of their children. Ted Bundy handed out photos of his five-year-old daughter to his prison visitors to show he wasn't a monster. The photos often proved effective. "He was very much the *Leave It to Beaver* dad: firm, fair, and gentle," recalls a lawyer from his defense team.

Though they might try to convey that impression, serial killers are never *Leave It to Beaver* dads. They might enjoy having their kids around from time to time, but they're incapable of putting their welfare first. Serial killer Gary Ridgway provides a chilling example: One night, Ridgway drove through the red light district of Seattle, with three-year old Matthew, strapped in his child seat. After Ridgway picked up a prostitute, he drove to a secluded location. Leaving his son alone in the dark, Ridgway and his victim walked into the woods. When the serial killer returned to the car, the little boy asked where the lady was. His father replied that she had decided to walk home. After Ridgway's arrest, detectives asked him what would have happened if Matthew had left the car and gone into the woods in time to witness the murder. "I would have had to kill him," the Green River Killer stated matter-of-factly.

Serial killers have also used their children as props. Ridgway took Matthew on his hunt because he knew the avalanche of publicity about a "Green River Killer" who trolled the Pacific Highway South between Tacoma and Seattle, was frightening prostitutes working that stretch. He thought his prey would be more likely to get into his vehicle if he had a child on board.

In 1973, Lucy Partington, age 21, was waiting for a bus in Gloucester, England, when serial killers Fred and Rosemary West pulled up and offered her a lift. Seeing that Rosemary was holding an infant, Lucy got in. The novelist

Martin Amis reflected on the deception. "My cousin Lucy was a very studious, religious, and brilliant girl," he says. "She was very sensible. Fred West got her into that car because he had his wife sitting next to him and she had a baby on her lap. He said, 'We'll run you home to your village—don't wait for the last bus.'" Lucy was held captive and murdered at the Wests' suburban home in Cheltenham.

CHAPTER 9

At Your Front Door

*"They would let me right into their house, and
once I was inside, they had no chance."*
—Serial killer David Gore

Sometimes all the predator had to do to gain entry to his victim's home was to ring the doorbell.

Why did the victim open her door? In some cases, it was because she was expecting someone else. In other instances, she was inquisitive. Criminal profiler Pat Brown says that occurs a lot, because "There is some odd human curiosity that drives us to want to know who is on the other side."

Sometimes the person outside was vaguely familiar, perhaps a neighbor. "Don't open the door unless you are expecting the person on the other side," cautions Candice DeLong. The former FBI special agent continues, "These rules do not apply only to strangers. Remember that virtually every rapist, killer, and child molester is somebody's neighbor, and plenty of them reside in ordinary suburban neighborhoods."

Once the door opens, some predators push their way inside. Most, however, wait for an invitation. It is only after the predator crosses the threshold and confirms the victim is alone in the house, that he drops his ruse.

Case History: The Boston Strangler

Albert DeSalvo had surveilled the house a few times. He knew the husband worked the late shift, and so the wife would be home alone. At nine p.m. promptly, DeSalvo rang the doorbell.

When the door opened, DeSalvo, pretending to be a concerned neighbor, described to the woman how he had been driving past when he noticed a peeping Tom staring into one of her windows. Naturally, she was alarmed, and when DeSalvo offered to come in and take a look around, the grateful woman let him in. It was only when the stranger inquired what time her husband was due back that she became suspicious. Thinking quickly, she ran to a room and locked herself in.

After a while, DeSalvo decided to leave. Hearing the front door close, the woman went to the window. She saw DeSalvo get in his car, and before he drove away, she jotted down the license plate number. Then she called police. The Boston Strangler was arrested later that night.

Often predators claimed to be on professional business. "I said, 'I am a real-estate agent' to get into the house," Michael Lee Lockhart told his prison psychiatrist. The ruse had come to him when he noticed, "there was an empty house next door." Mike DeBardeleben once posed as a Secret Service agent. After flashing a fake ID, he told Gayle Campbell that her former next-door neighbor was under investigation. Indicating the folder under his arm, he asked if he could come in and show her some photos.

Lieutenant Daniel Villanueva from the Miami Dade Police Impersonator Unit says that these days a lot of predators "use the guise of being a police officer to knock on a door." If the victim "lowers their guard just for a second, at that point, it's too late." Sometimes—rarely—the predator has been a real cop. Deputy sheriff Gore was in uniform when he rang the doorbell, and his police cruiser was parked outside. "I am so adamant now to warn people not to trust even someone they think is a cop," the serial killer declares without a trace of irony. "The majority of my victims, I got right inside their home." Lieutenant Villanueva urges that a woman living alone should not let a cop in if she isn't expecting the visit. "Call 911 or the local police station for verification."

Sometimes, the intruder had an appointment. Bobby Joe Long scoured local newspapers, looking for individuals advertising items for sale. Known to Florida police as the "Classified Ad Rapist," Long would phone during the daytime, hoping to catch women when their husbands were at work. If a woman answered, he would ask if he could come around to inspect the sale item. If he found she was alone, he would rape her. If there were other adults present, he'd inspect the item for sale and say he wasn't interested. Long raped more than fifty women in California and Florida.

Serial killers Alton Coleman and Debra Brown noticed a For Sale sign on the camper parked outside a home in Norwood, Ohio. When Marlene and Harry Walters opened the front door, the spree killers expressed interest in buying the camper. Unfortunately, rather than conduct business outside, the elderly couple invited the prospective buyers into their home. The Walters were murdered shortly afterwards.

Apartment Buildings

If you live in an apartment building, keep your door locked at all times, even if you're just stepping out to collect your mail or to visit the laundry room. A neighbor might have buzzed someone in who at that very moment is searching for an unlocked door. "Do you know the number of cases I have where the pizza delivery man gets in, delivers to 25D, and then tries the other doors on the way out?" commented a New York sex crimes prosecutor.

In 2013, Cesar Lucas delivered a pizza to a customer in a luxury high-rise on the Upper West Side of Manhattan, then the sixteen-year-old employee went looking for an unlocked door. He let himself into Kia Graves's apartment. He raped the actress while her seven-year-old daughter slept beside her in the bed. Despite his youth, the detectives who arrested Lucas found it wasn't his first sexual assault.

Luring a Victim Away from Her Home

Some predators attempt to entice their prey outside the home. Texas courtroom deputy Shannon LaForge remembers a case where a woman heard a crying baby on her porch: "She called the police because it was late and she thought it was weird. The police officer told her that they thought a serial killer had recorded a baby's cry and was using it to lure women out of their homes." In Louisiana, Derrick Todd Lee, known as the Baton Rouge Serial Killer, also used a recording of a crying baby to lure women outside their front door.

Gary Taylor created fake emergencies. On one occasion he phoned a victim, pretending there was a fire at her office. When he saw the woman hurrying to her car, Taylor overpowered her, and dragged her into his vehicle. David Gore says he became skilled at blindsiding female residents. "I've abducted women right out of their homes. I've spent days planning an abduction and then doing it. Women would come up missing, and no clues."

Scenario

A stranger knocks at the door. He claims he needs to make an urgent phone call. Should you let him inside your home? The answer is obviously no. But what if you believe it might genuinely be a life-or-death emergency? (Predators can be very convincing.) Then tell him that you'll call 911 for him. Never let him cross your threshold.

What if it's a neighbor who says he requires help? A neighbor you have seen around, but don't know well enough to trust? Predators have raped and killed their neighbors before. Dennis Rader, Russell Williams, and Albert DeSalvo murdered women from their neighborhoods. Kenneth Bianchi lured a neighbor from her apartment by pretending his car had just hit hers in a fender-bender accident. Candice DeLong was a head FBI field-profiler in California at the time. She remembers, "Ironically, she had just gotten off the phone with her mother, having assured her that she had securely locked the door because the Hillside Strangler was on the loose."

Neighborly etiquette doesn't require you to let anyone you don't know well into your home. However, if you're worried it might be a genuine emergency, tell him you will call 911 and that he is welcome to wait on your porch until the cops arrive.

CHAPTER 10

The Lair

*FBI agent Robert Ressler: And you started perfecting
your technique of getting people back to the house?
Jeffrey Dahmer: It became the drive and focus
of my life, the only thing that gave me satisfaction.*

Just as a wild animal drags its prey to a hidden area of jungle or grassland, the human predator prefers a concealed site as the second crime scene. What place is more secure than his own home?

One in three serial killers bring victims back to their residences, businesses, or farms. John Wayne Gacy lured twenty-nine victims to his house. Team killers Charles Ng and Leonard Lake kept victims in a bunker next door to their remote cabin in the Sierra Nevada Mountains. Serial killers Joel Norris, Robert Hansen, Robert Pickton, and Gary Ridgway brought prostitutes back to their homes. Nineteen percent of sexual assaults happen in a residence that belongs to someone other than the victim. Many serial rapists—including lawyers, doctors, dentists, ministers, and rabbis—have used their professional offices as lairs.

While the advantages of using his home or office are clear— total privacy and control over the victim— the predator has to figure out how to get his victim there. Sometimes—as with hiring prostitutes or photographing models— he offers money. Sometimes the bait he uses is an offer of temporary employment on a farm or business. John Wayne Gacy enticed fifteen-year-old Robert Piest by offering good wages for a summer job at his contracting business. Robert accompanied Gacy back to his home office for a job interview. Wayne Williams, who committed the Atlanta Child Murders, posed as a talent scout for the music industry. The boys accompanied Williams to his home recording studio in the belief they were going there to record a demo.

The Internet has made it easier for predators to lure victims into their lairs. They are able to conceal their identity when they post job offers online or arrange a first date through sites like OkCupid or Match.com.

Case History: Mark Twitchell

In 2008, Mark Twitchell killed Johnny Altinger in his garage in Edmonton, Canada. The garage was also the set for his amateur horror movie.

The two men corresponded through an online dating site where Twitchell posed as a woman. After arranging to meet in person at Twitchell's home, Johnny Altinger had emailed a friend for directions. When Altinger didn't return from "the date," the friend became concerned and called 911. The police went to the address Altinger had given his friend and discovered his dismembered body.

When news of Johnny Altinger's murder hit the press, another man contacted the police. The story he told them suggested what might have befallen Altinger. This man had been lured to the garage a week prior. Upon entering the garage, he had been attacked by a male stranger in a hockey mask. The man had escaped, but he was so mortified by the risk he had taken in going to a stranger's home that he had told nobody of the attack.

Jeffrey Dahmer, a talented amateur photographer, offered young men money to pose for him in his apartment. Often the bait worked. Dahmer told Detective Robert Ressler "one out of three [men] that he met in malls would consent to come back to his place and be photographed, while in the gay bars the proportion was two out of three." Other homicidal shutterbugs with home studios have included Christopher Wilder, William Bradford, and Murray Glatman.

Some predators just book a room. Serial killers Richard Cottingham and Christopher Wilder turned motel rooms into their lairs. Philip Markoff (Boston's Craigslist Killer) chose more upscale accommodation. He booked escorts online who visited him at the Westin and Marriott hotels. Lairs have also been created out of extremely low-rent destinations. "I had a trailer, and I turned it into my lair," David Gore recalled. Serial rapist Phillip Garrido once held a victim captive in a rented storage locker that he had outfitted with a bed. Years later, Garrido would confine Jaycee Dugard to a hut in his backyard.

Case History: John Wayne Gacy

John Wayne Gacy was extremely popular in his neighborhood of Des Plaines, Illinois, near Chicago. He always looked out for his neighbors. One of them remembers that Gacy "was always available for any chore, washing windows, setting up chairs for meetings—even fixing someone's leaky faucet. I don't know anyone who didn't like him." He was an active member of the wider community. As well as running a prosperous construction company, Gacy was captain of the local chapter of the Democratic Party, and he co-coordinated an event for twenty thousand people of Polish descent. He did volunteer work, too. Gacy performed regularly at children's hospitals as Pogo the Clown. No one who knew him guessed that underneath the guise of the jolly clown there was a sadistic killer.

Between 1972 and 1978, Gacy murdered thirty-three teenage boys and young men whom he had enticed to his home with offers of cash, if they were gay prostitutes, or jobs, if they sought employment. He would impress his victims by producing a photo of himself and the First Lady, Rosalynn Carter in 1978. Then Gacy would offer to show them his handcuff trick. Only those who refused to be handcuffed walked away alive from that house of horrors. The others—more trusting—were raped, tortured, and murdered.

Celebrity Lairs

Due to a false sense of familiarity, some victims felt comfortable letting down their guard with a celebrity, and overlooked the fact he was a complete stranger. Lana Clarkson must have been flattered when Phil Spector, the famous music producer, invited her home for a nightcap. Everyone in LA knew of Spector's collaborations with legendary rock-and-roll artists like John Lennon, the Rolling Stones and Leonard Cohen, but not many knew Spector had a history of threatening women with guns. Today Spector is in jail for Lana's murder.

Serial rapist Joseph Brooks parlayed his fame as an Academy Award-winning composer into enticing actresses to his Manhattan apartment for an "audition." When film director Roman Polanski hired thirteen-year-old Samantha Geimer to pose for photos for *Vogue* magazine, the girl's mother had no qualms about leaving her daughter alone with him. After plying Samantha with Champagne and drugs, the film director repeatedly raped her.

Case History: Joseph Brooks

Joseph Brooks, a Hollywood composer, achieved stardom when "You Light Up My Life," won the Golden Globe and the Academy Award for Best Original Song in 1977. He had also produced and directed the 1977 movie of the same title. The song was a huge hit. Debby Boone's version of "You Light Up My Life," was the most successful single of the 1970s in the United States.

Joseph Brooks used his credentials as a Hollywood director and producer to lure victims. Brooks's MO was to post an audition notice on Craigslist inviting actresses aged between eighteen and thirty to try out for a role in his next film.

In June 2009, he was arrested on charges of drugging and raping eleven women in his Manhattan apartment. Most were visiting from the West Coast. Brooks's longtime assistant Shawni Lucier made their flight and hotel arrangements, knowing full well what Brooks's intentions were. In 2011, Lucier pleaded guilty to ten counts of criminal facilitation, but Joseph Brooks was never brought to justice. He committed suicide before his trial date.

Held Captive

Okay, worst case scenario. What if you're trapped inside a predator's home? Is it game over? No. Your chance to escape might be just around the corner. Never give up hope. Amanda Berry, Lisa McVey, Elizabeth Smart, Katie Beers, Cynthia Vigil, Linda Grover and Debra Puglisi managed to escape their captivity.

Scrutinize your surroundings for something you could use as a weapon. If he places his gun down, you might be able to shoot him. If he turns his back, you could hit him over the head with a heavy object. Or you might be able to attract attention. Nineteen-year-old Linda Grover escaped Christopher Wilder by locking herself in the motel bathroom, pounding the walls, and screaming for help. Once the neighbors started assembling in the corridor, Wilder grabbed his suitcase and fled.

While considering your options for escape, act submissively so that the captor will eventually relax his guard. If possible, start to build a rapport with him like Lisa McVey did with Bobby Joe Long.

Case History: Lisa McVey

Although she was only seventeen, Lisa knew how to appease a rage-fueled personality. She had grown up in an abusive home. So, over the twenty-six hours Bobby Joe Long held her captive, Lisa appeared calm and empathetic. She was a good listener. She showed respect. Her obedient behavior acknowledged that Long was the one with the power. Now a police officer, Lisa McVey remembers: "It was 'Yes, Sir,' 'No, Sir.'"

Her submissive behavior was rewarded. The serial killer and his victim were watching Airwolf, which they agreed was their favorite TV show, when Long suddenly blurted out, "I don't know why I did this, you're such a nice girl." Bobby Joe Long untied Lisa, and then he showered and dressed her. He led her blindfolded to his car. Eventually, they stopped in a parking lot, and Long freed her, with instructions not to take off her blindfold until he was gone. Once she heard him drive away, Lisa McVey contacted the police.

Unbeknownst to her abductor, Lisa had been peeking underneath her blindfold, trying to memorize every detail she could about the interior of his car and the route they took. Because she provided such valuable clues to Long's identity, the police made a quick arrest. Once his identity was revealed, Lisa McVey learned that in the previous eight months, her kidnapper had murdered at least ten women in the Tampa Bay area. Thanks to McVey's level-headedness and resourcefulness, a shockingly brutal sexual predator would spend the rest of his life in jail.

CHAPTER 11

Predators On The Highway

*"Most girls who are taken away in cars and
vans are never seen alive again."*
—CRIMINAL PROFILER PAT BROWN

Serial killers watch bus stations, airports, and train stations for weary and disoriented female travelers. They troll areas where cruise ships dock; they sit in bars at airports and hotel resorts. Gerard Schaefer said he picked his prey from among "the many women who flock to Miami and Fort Lauderdale for the winter months."

On the FBI's list of serial killers' most targeted victims, "Women traveling alone— of all ages" was number three. But the location where travelers are most at risk wasn't as exotic as a hotel resort or cruise ship. It was the road. Serial killer David Gore recollects: "Many times I would just be simply driving uptown and I'd pass a car on the road with a woman by herself in it, and I'd turn to follow her to see where she went. And if she drove to someplace secluded, she became a target."

Before a predator like Gore takes to the highway, he packs what is known as his "kill kit." Typical items include duct tape, handcuffs, plastic ties, rope, a shovel, plastic sheeting, black garbage bags, and a weapon of some kind.

Sometimes the weapon is a knife or gun, but often it's something less deadly like a screwdriver, hammer, tire iron, crowbar, or lug wrench.

An Example of a Kill Kit
After Ted Bundy's arrest, detectives found a gym bag on the front seat of his Volkswagen.

It contained the following items: a rope; two gloves of different makes; a pair of panty hose with holes cut out for the eyes, mouth, and nose; a pair of handcuffs; a flashlight; strips cut from a sheet; and a box of black garbage bags. Lying next to the gym bag, there was an ice pick, a crowbar, and a ski mask.

In an FBI study of thirty sexual sadists, twelve described themselves as "compulsive" drivers. Serial rapist Barry Simonis said driving provided a sense of "freedom from responsibility." He told Roy Hazelwood that he once drove more than eighty thousand miles in eight months. Ted Bundy drove his VW through the states of Washington, California, Oregon, Nevada, Utah, and Colorado in search of victims. Randy Woodfield, dubbed the I-5 Killer, drove back and forth along the Interstate 5 corridor. He picked up victims in Washington, Oregon, and California.

Team Killers
Some weekends, David Gore teamed up with his cousin Fred Waterfield. "One of us would pick the other up early, and we'd literally drive hundreds of miles, hunting," Gore recollected fondly. It is not unusual for predators to hunt in pairs. In the 1990s, Dr. Eric W. Hickey, a criminologist, conducted a survey of over four hundred serial killers. Fifteen percent of them had partnered with another killer. Two-thirds of the teams consisted of two males; one-third of the teams consisted of a male and a female killer. The biggest advantage to taking a partner along is that one predator can control the victim while the other predator drives.

Some male team killers met in prison, like Roy Norris and Lawrence Bittaker. Others were family members. The Hillside Stranglers, Angelo Buono and Kenneth Bianchi, were cousins, like Gore and Waterfield. Male team killers include Leonard Lake and Charles Ng; Dean Corll and Elmer Wayne Henley; Christopher Worrell and James Miller; and Henry Lee Lucas and Ottis Toole.

When a male and female predator hit the road together, the male is usually the dominant partner. Initially the female's role is to lure the prey, like Myra Hindley did for Ian Brady or Carol Bundy did for Douglas Clark. Charlene Gallego enticed teenage girls into the vehicle by inviting them to smoke a joint; then she would point a gun at them while her husband Gerald raped them. Since the females were eager accomplices, eventually they insisted on playing a bigger role. Karla Homolka quickly progressed from luring victims for her husband Paul Bernardo to actively participating in their rape, torture and death.

Case History: Karla Homolka and Paul Bernardo.

Known in Canada as the Ken and Barbie Killers, this good-looking Ontario couple was engaged when they started raping and killing teenage girls. Their first victim— Homolka's sister Tammy— was fourteen when Karla, who was six years older, drugged her and presented her to Paul as a "gift." Tammy died of a drug overdose. The couple married several months later.

While Tammy's death was probably unintentional, the next death was not. Leslie Mahaffy was sitting outside her Burlington house, having been locked out, when Paul Bernado kidnapped her. She wasn't quite fifteen. Kristen French was abducted several months later. Homolka had approached the fourteen-year-old girl and asked for directions. Kristen obligingly accompanied the pretty twenty-two year old blonde back to the car, where Homolka spread a map over the roof. As the two females conferred, Bernardo crept up behind Kristin. After he pushed her into the backseat, Homolka scrambled in beside the girl and leveled a gun at her. They drove her to their home.

Despite Homolka's courtroom plea that she had been too frightened to disobey her husband, videotapes revealed that Homolka had been an enthusiastic partner in crime rather than the battered woman she claimed to be.

Behavioral profilers say that the kind of female who finds it exciting to hunt alongside her mate is usually a psychopath. Other male-female serial killing teams have included Fred and Rosemary West; Martha Beck and Raymond Fernandez; Charlie Starkweather and Caril Ann Fugate; and Alton Coleman and Debra Brown.

Case History: Colleen Stan

Colleen Stan started hitchhiking south from Eugene, Oregon, on May 19, 1977. She was trying to get to a friend's birthday party in the northern Californian hamlet of Westwood. Colleen figured she should be extremely careful about the lift she took, and the 19-year-old girl let several cars go by. Before too long, a blue Dodge Colt pulled over. She saw a couple close to her own age sitting up in front. The young woman was holding a baby on her lap. Colleen was reassured they would be a safe choice. She ran over and climbed into the backseat.

But as time passed, this mild-mannered couple began to seem more sinister. The man kept staring at her through the rear-view mirror. Those glances made Colleen uncomfortable. Why was he looking at her instead of the beautiful scenery they were passing through? When they stopped for gas, Colleen's intuition urged her to flee, but since she couldn't put her finger on why she felt uneasy, and she needed the lift to get to the party, she dismissed her intuition.

It was a decision she would always regret. Colleen Stan never made it to the party. For the next seven years, she would be the sex slave of Cameron and Janice Hooker, and sleep in a box under their bed.

The Predator's Vehicle

"In the early 1970s, VW Beetles seemed to be the car of choice for serial killers," says John Douglas, who retired from the FBI in 1995. Douglas explains that was because Volkswagens were reputed to get more miles to the gallon, an important consideration for serial killers who frequently crossed state lines. Another reason that serial killers preferred VWs, as Ted Bundy told detectives, was that "you can take out the front seat." It was helpful, said Bundy, because "it's easier to carry cargo in them. You can control it better."

At the end of the '70s, Volkswagens were replaced as the serial killer's favorite vehicle. "After VWs, we were starting to see a shift in vehicle of preference to vans," Douglas remembers. Today, the most popular vehicle is a van with darkened windows. "Unlike a car, in the back of a van you can do whatever you want and not be seen," says Douglas. "You have, in effect, a mobile murder site."

Of course, not every serial killer drives a van. Some, like Gary Ridgway (the Green River Killer), drive the family sedan, or, in Jerry Brudos's case, the family station wagon. Edmund Kemper drove a yellow Ford Galaxy.

The Police Car

Nine of the thirty sexual sadists in his study were "police buffs," says Roy Hazelwood. "They collected police paraphernalia and drove vehicles that resembled police cruisers." During the years he ran the FBI's Crime Investigative Analysis Program, the trend became so widespread says John Douglas that "one of the things we began saying in some of our profiles was that the UNSUB would drive a police-like vehicle."

Mike DeBardeleben adapted his blue Thunderbird to resemble a police cruiser by adding a police scanner, a two-way radio, a siren under the grille, and official-looking police lights. Wayne Williams drove an actual police cruiser that had been stripped down and sold at auction.

Scenario

A police car is following you, and the "officer" indicates you should pull off the road. Police say that even if the driver is a police officer, no action will be taken against you for being cautious. Just signal to show that you are aware of him, and then drive slowly to a well-lit and populated location. Call 911 on your cell phone and explain your predicament. If the cop approaches, don't roll down your window all the way. Open it just a fraction, and inform him you have called 911 to verify his identity.

Case History: Mike DeBardeleben

Serial killer Mike DeBardeleben had modified his blue Thunderbird to resemble a police vehicle. He installed red lights and a siren. Inside there was a scanner and a two-way radio. His MO was to flash his lights and pull a woman driver over. DeBardeleben would then pull out his fake police badge and inform the driver that she resembled a female robber for whom the police had just issued an all-points bulletin. He would handcuff her and place in his car, then drive to a preselected location.

Michelle Wallace survived one such abduction attempt. She told detectives that ordinarily her car doors and windows would have been unlocked, but on this occasion, "there had been some recent assaults on women in New Jersey and my mom was on my back." Luckily, the young woman had locked her doors and windows.

When DeBardeleben flashed his lights, Michelle Wallace obligingly pulled the car over. But as the police officer got out of his cruiser and approached, she decided to exercise caution. When the cop knocked on her window, she made sure to roll the window down just a little. Even that was too much. When the cop demanded to see her license and registration, Michelle turned to retrieve her purse from the backseat, and that's when the man's arm shot through the window. DeBardeleben managed to unlock the car door and pull it open. Michelle struggled to pull the door closed, in a dangerous tug of war.

"I braced one foot on the brake and one hand on the steering wheel and one hand on the horn. He couldn't move me." The two battled furiously until another driver arrived at the scene. DeBardeleben fled.

Never Get in the Car!

Criminal profilers agree that a woman should resist—even at the risk of severe injury—being pushed into a stranger's vehicle. Pat Brown explains: "The kind of predator who takes a girl away in a vehicle tends to have more elaborate plans than the guy who jumps out from behind the bush. These are sexually sadistic killers." In the words of one woman who managed to escape: "Never ever get into a vehicle with anyone you don't know, even if he says he has a gun or the gun is pointed at you. Run, scream, and do anything else to bring attention to yourself. If he is going to kill or hurt you, take your chances and let him do it right there, where there is a greater chance of having witnesses. Don't let there be a crime scene out in an isolated area where nobody can help you."

Even if he has a deadly weapon, your chances of survival are better if you fight back forcefully. If a predator tries to push you into his vehicle, cling to the outside. If your back is pressed against the car, kick him hard in the testicles, or grasp them and twist until he falls to the ground in agony. You can also do real damage by attacking his eyes, nose, or ears. Fighting dirty is a safer option than being driven away in a van. I will give you detailed instructions in a later chapter.

The Front Passenger Seat

If he manages to drag you into his car, remain on the offensive. A kidnapper needs to restrain his victim in order to drive. Resist if he tries to handcuff you or bind your hands with plastic ties. You'll have more options if your hands remain free. You could make him swerve by grabbing the wheel. You could grab the wheel and crash the car into a tree, or make it jump a median strip. You could alert other drivers by leaning on the horn. And if there is an opportunity to yank the car door open, you could throw yourself outside, which is how eighteen-year-old Carol Da Ronch escaped.

Though Ted Bundy managed to force the girl's right wrist into a handcuff, he couldn't get hold of Carol's left wrist because she was struggling, screaming, hitting, and scratching him. When Carol reached for the door handle, Bundy pulled out a gun and threatened her: "I will blow your brains out," but Carol Da Ronch didn't listen. She kicked free of him, opened the door, and fell out of the car. When Bundy jumped out, he was wielding a crowbar. Da Ronch kicked Bundy in the groin and broke free and ran into the road, one handcuff still hanging from her wrist. She was rescued by passing motorists.

Waving through the Taillight

But what if the abductor locks you in his trunk? You can't throw yourself from the vehicle or crash it, so how will you escape? One way is by alerting other drivers to the fact you are a captive. Push your leg through the taillight—most of them are easy to smash— and wave it around. The other drivers will call 911 on their cell phones, but the kidnapper won't be able to see what you're up to.

But don't just wait for the sound of sirens. Check to see if there is an emergency release cord. If there is, and you can pop the trunk, wait until the vehicle slows down enough that you can roll out without killing yourself or being run over by a speeding vehicle. Once you're out, keeping low to the ground so the kidnapper won't notice you in his rearview mirror. Start running.

Case History: Jennifer Asbenson

Serial killer Andrew Urdiales forced Jennifer Asbenson, nineteen, into the trunk of his car. Afraid she was going to die, Asbenson prayed desperately. Suddenly, the fear passed and a fierce clarity took over. She began to search methodically for the trunk's release mechanism. When she found it, she waited for the right moment then she bailed out and ran. She tried flagging down several cars, but none would stop. Urdiales glimpsed her through his rearview mirror, and came running after her. Jennifer stood in the path of a navy truck, forcing it to stop. Urdiales fled. The marines took her to the police.

Search for a Weapon

There might be something inside the trunk that you can use as a weapon. Is there an LED light on your key chain? Does your cell phone have a flashlight app? If you can't see, then just feel around the trunk. One survivor found a sharp object, which she used to attack the predator when he opened the trunk. Another found a floor jack.

Nothing? Check your pockets. A kidnap victim once escaped by disabling the abductor with a safety pin.

CHAPTER 12

The Woman Driver

*"Women's liberation is another extraordinarily
interesting thing, because women have a great deal more
freedom to move here and there. They are no longer
stuck in their homes. They are not watched over."*
—SERIAL KILLER TED BUNDY

f you're planning to drive a long distance, it might seem smarter to drive at
night when the roads are quiet, but highway security experts recommend
you don't. Profiler Pat Brown says: "I avoid driving lonely highways through
prairies at night." It's safer to drive in the daytime. Make sure your cell phone is
charged before you take to the road, and don't forget your charger. The best one
is the kind that plugs into the cigarette lighter.

Keep your gas gauge between medium and full. The experts suggest you keep
a container of gas in the trunk in case you run out somewhere remote. If a driver in
another lane indicates something is wrong with your car, head straight to the nearest service station, or, if it's late at night, another twenty-four-hour business. If the
other driver follows you, don't get out of your car until he has driven off.

Reduce the risk of a breakdown with regular tune-ups.

Roadside Emergencies

If your car stalls, turn your hazard lights on, lock the doors, close the windows
all the way, and call 911. Predators zero in on women motorists in need of help.
David Gore couldn't believe his luck when he saw a woman standing beside a

vehicle with its hood up: "I pulled over and offered to help and she accepted. Since her car had a busted radiator hose, I told her I could drive her to an auto parts store, get the hose, and come back and fix it." After the woman got into Gore's truck, she was never seen alive again.

If you're experiencing car trouble and there is no garage in sight, head for a populated and well-lit area, like a twenty-four-hour business. Call 911 or AAA.

Case History: Jerry Brudos

Jerry Brudos used to drive his station wagon along the I-5 freeway, from Portland to Salem to Corvallis, trolling for victims. In November 1968, he saw Jan Whitney standing by her broken-down car, and pulled over. Brudos inspected the engine. He told her he knew what was wrong.

"I offered to fix her car, but I didn't have my tools with me. I said I'd take her back," he said. Perhaps reassured by the sight of children's toys on the backseat, Jan got into Brudos's vehicle. Once they arrived at his house, Brudos dragged Jan Whitney into the garage and murdered her.

Scenario

You need roadside assistance but your cell phone is dead. You can't call 911 or AAA. You can't text anyone. Then a man gets out of his vehicle. He approaches to offer help. This is the first car you've seen in an hour. Do you really have to refuse his offer?

Here is a pretty low risk strategy. Open your window a tiny crack. Thank the stranger. Tell him that you have already called 911 but you would appreciate it if he made a follow-up call.

In Need of Assistance?

When possible, it's always better to *choose* the person to help you. Preferably a woman, says security expert Gavin de Becker. "Is what I've said politically incorrect? Maybe so. I don't care if it's politically incorrect. The fact is that men in all cultures, at all times and at all times in history are more violent than women—and facts are not political."

What If Your Vehicle Won't Start?

Predators disable women's cars by removing the car's rotor, or distributor cap, and then they watch from a distance. If you've returned to a parking lot to find your vehicle won't start, be wary of the man who suddenly shows up, offering to take a look under the hood. Get your help from AAA or 911 instead. As you settle down to wait for them, make sure your doors are locked and the windows are closed.

Case History: "Vikky"

Having just enjoyed a pleasant evening with friends at the local tavern, Vikky walked across the parking lot to her car. But when she put the key in the ignition, Vikky was surprised to find that the engine didn't respond. Not wanting to persevere in the cold, she returned to the tavern and asked a friend to give her a lift home. Vikky returned to the vehicle at dawn, but she still couldn't get it to start. When a young man emerged from behind the tavern and offered to help, Vikky gratefully accepted. She recalls: "It didn't occur to me then that he might have deliberately disabled my car." It was only later that the police "found that someone had pulled the distributor cap."

The young man failed to get Vikky's car started, but volunteered: "I know someone who has jumpers." So they both set off in his VW, which had been parked nearby. They were chatting pleasantly when "All of a sudden the guy pulled a switchblade from between his legs and held it to my neck." Vikky fought furiously and managed to escape. She filed a report with police, but they couldn't find the man who threatened her life. A year later the young woman saw him again: "I was watching the news on television, and I saw the man on screen. I yelled to my friend, 'Look! That's him. That's the guy who almost killed me.' When they said his name, it was Ted Bundy."

A Flat Tire

Another favorite predatory trick is to deflate tires. If you discover your car has a flat tire, be skeptical of the man who volunteers to change it. If you need assistance, call AAA or 911 instead. As well as deflating tires, predators have also punctured them by scattering glass across the road.

Robert Leroy Anderson of South Dakota made small, sharp triangles he referred to as "tire poppers." He painted them to blend in with the road surface so that it would be difficult for a driver to see them at night. Anderson enlisted his friend Jamie Hammer to help with his plan. He told Hammer to stand by the side of the road and wait for his call via two-way radio. Anderson would be sitting in a vehicle farther up the road, keeping watch for a lone woman traveler. Once he spotted a suitable target, he would describe her car to Hammer over the two-way radio. That was the cue for Hammer to arrange the poppers across the road. Anderson would follow the woman in his vehicle—picking up Hammer en route—until her tire went flat, forcing her to stop. He would offer her his assistance.

Being Followed

What should you do if another driver is shadowing you? Call 911 on your cell phone, and inform the operator of your suspicions. Head to the nearest police station or firehouse, or drive to a twenty-four-hour business and wait for the police. If you don't have your cell phone and can't call 911, drive to the nearest gas station. If the vehicle follows you into the station, do not get out of the car. Honk the horn, and ask the attendant to call 911.

Waiting for the light to change

Security experts say you should approach red lights with caution, keeping a good distance from the car ahead. Keep an eye on the cars beside and behind you. If a stranger approaches your vehicle while you're waiting for the lights to change, check that the doors are locked. If he appears to be a police officer, just open the window a tiny crack to speak to him. If he's bogus, you don't want him pushing his arm through the window to unlock the door.

If the stranger produces a gun and threatens to shoot through the glass if you don't open the door, step on the gas. Your car is a one-ton weapon, so use it to knock the stranger out of the way if you have to. Get out of there by going forward or backward. If you can do it safely, run the red light. If you can't move, blast your horn to attract attention.

If a vehicle behind bumps your car, don't assume it's an accident. When the other driver approaches, open your window just a crack to take his information.

If your instinct tells you there is something wrong, forget any conversation about insurance. Drive away once the light turns green. "Dents are easy to fix," as FBI profiler Candice DeLong points out.

Carjackings

If a carjacker demands your keys, hand them over to him without comment and quickly walk away from the scene. Leave it to the police to get your vehicle back. But if the carjacker jumps in beside you and commands you to drive, it's likely you are his real target—not your car. It is better to deliberately crash or throw yourself from your moving vehicle than to drive both of you to an isolated crime scene. A woman once escaped serial killers Alton Coleman and Debra Brown by driving her car into a parked truck, then jumping out and running away.

To avoid carjackings, AAA advises drivers not to get out of the vehicle in an isolated area to use an ATM, pay phone, or newspaper dispenser.

Escaping the Trunk of Your Own Car

Sometimes a carjacker locks the driver in the trunk of her vehicle. Ask your mechanic to demonstrate how to trip the latch. Practice getting in and out of the trunk of your car. (Have a friend standing outside.) Keep a flashlight in the trunk for illuminating dark corners. (Don't forget to periodically check that its batteries are still working.) Some trunks have an emergency release cord. If you're unsure how yours works, ask the mechanic to show you.

What should you put in the trunk for self-defense? Mace or pepper spray, because you'd be able to spray it into a predator's eyes once he stopped the car and opened the trunk. A tire-iron is an obvious choice. A small air horn could be used as a freeze-spray when turned upside down. And so on. Use your imagination.

CHAPTER 13

Looking Through Your Window

"Once he becomes comfortable with breaking and entering, he may then escalate to rape. If he realizes he could be identified by his victim if he doesn't take preventative action, rape can end in murder."
—FBI CRIMINAL PROFILER JOHN DOUGLAS

At the Behavioral Science Unit, there is a saying: "Not all peeping Toms are rapists, but all rapists are peeping Toms." It applies to serial killers, too. Now an associate professor of Criminal Justice at the University of New Haven, ex-homicide detective, Robert Keppel interrogated more than fifty serial killers including Ted Bundy and Gary Ridgway. He found that without exception, "Every serial killer started as a voyeur first."

John Douglas discovered the same thing: "I am in no way implying every peeping Tom (or even most) ends up as a serial killer," but two decades at the BSU showed him "Certain behaviors can be stepping stones to rape. In case after case, we have been able to chart the progression."

Ted Bundy was fifteen when he began peeping into women's windows. Some peeping Toms take photos of women undressing; others masturbate while they watch women going about their business. Bundy did the latter. "I developed a preference for what they call autoerotic sexual activity" is how Bundy described it.

When peeping loses its thrill, the next step for a budding sex predator is crossing the threshold of the victim's home and stealing a trophy, usually a bra or panties. As a youth, Dennis Rader pretended to be a spy while he sneaked around a stranger's house. Rummaging through her underwear drawer felt "vaguely sexual." David Gore was another teenage thief. "I used to love to enter women's homes when they weren't there," he remembers. "I found true pleasure in seeing things they didn't want people to see."

Albert DeSalvo started breaking in at fourteen: "There was something exciting, thrilling about going into somebody's home. It had to do with going into the bedrooms where women had been sleeping, or were sleeping, and there were times I would get an erection just standing there outside the bedroom door listening to some woman breathe." Rape was inevitable according to DeSalvo: "It was only a matter of time before I would feel strong and tough enough to go into the bedroom where the woman was and make her do what I wanted with her."

Secure the Blinds

The most effective way to deter a peeping Tom is obvious: give him nothing to look at. Close your blinds at night. Also, create a prowler-free zone. If you live in a house, plant small, thorny bushes outside the exterior windows (rose bushes, for example). If you are an apartment dweller, place thorny plants on the windowsill. (Flowering cactuses are also pretty.)

If you hear a suspicious noise outside your house, turn on the exterior lights, call 911, and then call your next-door neighbors (if you have close neighbors) and ask them to turn on their lights as well. Those simple steps will cause most peeping Toms to leave.

Case History: Colonel Russell Williams

As the commander of Canada's largest air force base, Colonel Russell Williams lived in nearby Belleville, Ontario. This highly decorated military officer flew the plane that brought Queen Elizabeth and Prince Philip to Canada. But despite a distinguished career, there was a dark side to the colonel. During nightly runs,

William liked to peer through the windows of his female neighbors. Sometimes, when the occupant was out, Williams broke in and stole items of lingerie. Colonel Russell Williams eventually admitted to having committed eighty-two of these fetish burglaries, but he had done far worse.

In November 2009, he broke into the home of Marie Comeau, a thirty-eight-year-old corporal serving under his command, where he raped and killed her. Soon afterwards, he gained entry to the home of Jessica Lloyd, aged twenty-seven. He raped and asphyxiated the young woman. In 2011, Williams pleaded guilty to those two homicides as well as two sexual assaults. Today, the commander has been stripped of military honors and occupies a jail cell in Kingston, Ontario. Police suspect he has committed many more rapes than those to which he has currently confessed.

Get Rid of All Personal Information

A burglar wants to steal money and goods. Keen to avoid a confrontation with the resident, he breaks in during the day when she is at work. A sex predator is excited by the invasion itself. He prefers to operate at night, usually after the occupant has gone to bed. His purpose is to sexually assault her.

What makes the predator choose one residence over another? First, he looks for evidence of a single female occupant. Dennis Rader started "by checking her mailbox." Ted Bundy roamed his neighborhood checking "names on mailboxes." So, if you have a female name on your mailbox, take it off. (Two female names aren't necessarily a deterrent.) Other options? If you have to keep your name on the mailbox for some reason, use initials instead of a first name, or consider adding a male name.

Women need to cover up the fact they live alone, says Dennis Rader (BTK.)

"The most important thing they can do is give the impression that they live with a man. Maybe have some men's clothes scattered around or leave a toiletry kit out in the open, just in case someone breaks in to scope the place out." If the woman has an answering machine, Rader suggests she put a man's voice on the outgoing recording. Those signs of a male presence would have turned him away, he says.

The predator looks for indications he will encounter minimal resistance. A gun control sticker on a vehicle reassures him there are no guns in the house; a peace sign or a statue of Buddha in the garden suggests the resident will be easy to intimidate. A For Sale sign provides the perfect excuse to ring the doorbell.

Routines

Rader advises women to "be extra suspicious of vehicles they see parked out in front of their house or apartment." They should call the police. "What I am always looking for is routines," Rader explains. "I often used to drive back to my victims' houses over and over again and park out front."

To establish his target's daily routine, the predator might also follow her in his vehicle. In Nancy Fox's case, "I followed her a couple of times, " Dennis Rader says. "I went to Herzberg's where she worked. I knew when she got home." Once he had that information, Rader broke into Nancy's house and waited for her to return.

Police recommend that women who live alone or with small children, should not follow the same routine every day. For instance, switch the times you go to the gym or pick up mail or do grocery shopping. And for those patterns you can't change—for example, going to work—vary the roads you drive.

Case History: Joshua Komisarjevsky

When he was a teenager living in Cheshire, Connecticut, Joshua Komisarjevsky would watch a house for days, studying the residents' routines. Then he would cut a window screen and crawl through it, or sneak in through an unlocked French door. He could find his way through darkened rooms easily because he wore a pair of night-vision goggles. He stole things, of course, but he got a bigger kick from watching people sleep. "It's extremely high risk, and extremely brazen," he wrote in his journal, "but hey, my life is defined by risk."

At twenty-one, he was arrested and charged with breaking into nineteen homes. He received a nine-year sentence, but only served five years. Upon his release, Komisarjevsky was paroled to a halfway house, where he shared a room with career burglar Steven Hayes. Within a month, the two parolees were planning more robberies.

On July 22, 2007, Jennifer Hawke-Petit drove her daughters—seventeen-year-old Hayley and eleven-year-old Michaela— home from the Super Stop and Shop in Cheshire. They were unaware of the car following them. When the white

Mercedes turned into 300 Sorghum Mill Drive, the two men felt they had struck gold. The comfortable Petit home was secluded, set back from the street and partially surrounded by trees. The house was also on a corner lot, which would make it easier to sneak around unseen, and the trees would provide good cover.

Komisarjevsky and Hayes returned two nights later. They entered the Petit home through an unlocked door in the basement. When they reached the porch, they were surprised to see a man asleep in a recliner. Komisarjevsky checked inside to see if there were other males in residence. He didn't want to encounter "some seventeen-year-old high school wrestler," he explained later. Satisfied, he returned with a baseball bat and beat Dr. Petit into unconsciousness.

The intruders woke up the females and tied them up. At 9 a.m. Hayes drove Mrs. Petit to the bank, where she withdrew fifteen thousand dollars, then they returned to 300 Sorghum Mill Drive. Meanwhile Dr. Petit had regained consciousness. The badly beaten man crawled to a neighbor's house to call 911. But the police arrived too late. Komisarjevsky and Hayes had raped Mrs. Petit and Michaela, set the house on fire and fled. Tragically, the three captives perished.

If You're Away from Home During the Day

Dennis Rader advises that before heading to work, you should leave the impression the house is occupied. "It's a good idea to always leave the radio on in your home." Alternatively, buy a timing device that activates the TV. Another idea is to put the living room or kitchen lights on a timer, so they light up around dusk.

If an agitated pet greets you at the front door, it might indicate your home has been entered in your absence. A young co-ed who survived Ted Bundy's Chi Omega killing spree in Florida, speculated that Bundy had broken into the sorority house earlier that day. "We were all gone Saturday afternoon, even the housemother. The house was empty for a couple of hours. When we came home, the housemother's cat was acting spooked, and its hair was standing on end. It ran through our legs and out the door – and it didn't come back for two weeks."

Another red flag is if your pet doesn't run to greet you as usual, or doesn't respond to your call. Don't enter your residence. Phone your local police station. Or ask a male friend or trusted neighbor to help you check the house.

CHAPTER 14

Home Sweet Home

*"The confrontation is commonly the first or second
floor of a building, or a single family dwelling."*
—THE FBI'S NATIONAL CENTER FOR THE
ANALYSIS OF VIOLENT CRIME

All forty-one subjects in an FBI study of serial rapists reported they had eventually abandoned streets and alleys, believing it was safer to attack women in their own homes. As one rapist explained, "When I get her in that bedroom, there's four walls and me, and that's all there is."

Thirty-seven percent of rapes occur in the woman's home. This means, says Candice DeLong, a former FBI spokesperson on women's safety, that keeping doors and windows locked should be the first priority. "If they try a door or a window and find it locked," says DeLong, "they just move on to the house next door until they finally hit on someone who is easy prey."

Serial rapists usually prefer the first or second floors of apartment buildings, because they're easier to enter and exit quickly. While that doesn't mean you shouldn't move into that lovely garden apartment, you'll need to take extra precautions to secure it. In suburbs and towns, predators prefer single-family houses, particularly on large lots. Corner houses are particularly appealing because of the distance from neighbors. There are also effective ways to secure these homes, as you'll find out later.

Let's talk neighborhood. If you're thinking about moving into an unfamiliar neighborhood, do a drive-by at night. What might be a peaceful block during the day could be a hotbed of crime at night. It's also a good idea to go online and check the police blotter (the precinct's daily written record of arrests and incidents) for a list of recent crimes in the area.

But wherever you choose to live, the best way to deter a break-in is to make the predator believe that it will be no easy task to gain entry to your home.

Do Your Own Risk Analysis

Grab a notebook and survey the premises. How dark does your home get at night? Do you need extra lighting close to the house? Are your shades and curtains closed? Identify any areas where an intruder might hide himself, not only among trees and bushes but also in the garage. This is the kind of information that goes into a victimology report. The FBI calls these "location risk factors." If the shrubbery outside your windows is dense enough to hide someone, prune it back. Or get rid of the shrubs and substitute a flower garden.

If your home is on a large block of land, distant from neighbors, consider installing a motion detector. If you live on an isolated farm, try to get on first-name terms with the police in the nearest town. A nice way to introduce yourself is by dropping the police station with cookies, a pie, or a ham. When the local police conduct an annual coat drive, deliver the coats in person rather than just putting them in an outside collection bin. Make a contribution to their favorite charity. And if you like a particular cop, ask for his or her direct number. Put it on speed dial.

An Open Window

Most of us don't check the windows after a handyman has left. Always check. Sometimes a window—it's usually the bathroom window—is left open or unlocked because the handyman or his accomplice plans to return later.

What about sleeping with an open window? A woman living alone is taking a huge risk, unless she lives in a high-rise apartment with no exterior balcony or fire escape. But in the summer, it can be stifling without air-conditioning. What other options does she have?

There are some windows that can be fixed so the fresh air comes in but the opening is too small to crawl through. "You can easily secure double-hung windows," DeLong instructs, "by pounding a nail halfway into each side of the upper window's sash so that the bottom window can be raised only a few inches." If you don't have that kind of window, buy an electric fan, but don't wait until a heat wave, because the stores usually run out of them.

Donna Lynn Vetter, an FBI employee, was murdered during a Texas heat wave. The intruder had gained access through an open window. What follows is an extract from the FBI's victimology report. It provides some insight into what the FBI regards as high-risk and low-risk factors for women who live alone.

Case History: Donna Lynn Vetter

Donna Lynn Vetter worked as a stenographer for the FBI in San Antonio. . . . She was described as a quiet and hard-working introvert who rarely initiated conversation with fellow employees. Donna Vetter would have been considered less likely to be targeted as a victim when one considers characteristics that determine victim risk level. Her employment as an FBI stenographer; conservative dress and life-style (she did not frequent bars or nightclubs); total lack of alcohol use, drug use, and criminal history; modest income; and quiet withdrawn personality all contributed to this low-risk status. In addition her age and physical state (no handicaps) did not increase her vulnerability.

However, there were two factors that elevated her risk status. One was the location of her apartment: an industrialized and commercial area of a lower-income, blue-collar neighborhood. The second factor was her trusting attitude and lack of concern for her personal safety. She simply would smile at the concerns that fellow employees voiced over her lack of safety precautions. Vetter used fresh air through open windows and doors instead of the air conditioner in order to save electricity; in her mind, frugality was more of an issue in deciding where she had lived than was the possibility of rape or murder. It was this naïve and unsuspecting attitude that became a contributing factor to her death.

An Unlocked Door

Richard Ramirez was known as the Night Stalker. Ramirez wandered through various neighborhoods in Los Angeles and San Francisco, trying doors until he found an unlocked one. Serial killer Robert Browne followed the same pattern. As Browne told detectives, he just "rambled" around his neighborhood at night, checking the doors until he found one that opened.

Locking your doors is an important security measure but a lot of people don't do it. In the wake of the tragic Petit home invasion in Connecticut, community police officer Joe DeFelice gave this advice at a town hall meeting: "People who are going to commit crimes are going to do it. You have got to be prepared. There are simple things people can do, such as locking doors. Many people grew up in a society where they didn't lock their doors. I can't tell you how many calls I get where the people say, 'I never lock my doors.' Lock your doors!"

He added: "A burglar with a crowbar can easily lift a sliding glass door off its track. It's very easy to do." DeFelice advised the worried neighbors that to prevent a burglar entering through French doors, "you have to install quality deadbolts and use them properly." He warned, "a lot of times people will leave a key inside the deadbolt. That doesn't make a lot of sense." It was also a mistake to hide the house keys outside. "I can't tell you how many times I've gone to homes where there's a fake rock by the door. They are plastic rocks designed to hold keys, and they are supposed to blend in with the landscaping. A burglar with a trained eye can pick out the fake rock right away, and that makes it just so easy for someone to get into your home."

What Makes a Home Invader Move On?
Three things. 1. an alarm system. 2. a male resident. 3. a dog.

An alarm system:
Look for a good-quality one, with a siren loud enough to wake not only you but your closest neighbors, too. If your budget doesn't stretch to an alarm system, you can still post an "armed response" sticker in the window. Another idea is to rig up a homemade alarm. Some residents hang chimes in the bedroom window; others string aluminum cans together to hang from the door. (Use enough cans so that if someone opened the door, there would be a loud crashing.)

A man in residence:
Place men's sneakers or slippers, preferably large ones, outside your front door. You can pick up a worn pair from your local thrift store. If you hang washing

to dry on an outside line, purchase items of male clothing to intermingle with your own.

A dog:

Dogs are a huge turn-off. Career burglars surveying maps of the neighborhood, cross out the houses with dogs. Their size doesn't matter much. Chihuahuas can be as quick to attack as German Shepherds. Sex predators avoid such homes, too. It only takes some quick barks for an occupant to wake up. More frenzied bouts of barking will prompt neighbors to dial 911. Dennis Rader thought so highly of a canine's ability to deter "guys like me," he recommended a woman living alone "should get two dogs. One outside the house and one for inside."

No dog? No one needs to know that. Place a doggy water bowl at the back door—the bigger the better! —and a beware of dog sign on your front gate.

Serial killer Danny Rolling suggests women who live alone should take the following steps, because "Take it from me. It pays to be paranoid."

1. If your bedroom doesn't have a screen, get one and nail it to the windowsill.
2. Place a bunch of empty bottles in the windowsill.
3. Get some curtains.
4. Buy a deadbolt and put it on your bedroom door so you can lock yourself in.
5. Keep a loaded Magnum under the pillow. (Okay, I know. This is a very dangerous and stupid idea. We're going to ignore this one.)

Case History: Danny Rolling

Danny Rolling decided to become what he called a "superstar" among criminals. In August 1990, he murdered a family in Louisiana. Then he took a Greyhound bus to Gainesville, Florida, where he pitched a tent in the woods near the University of Florida campus. Over several days, Rolling broke into three different apartments near the campus. On the first day, he stabbed roommates Christine Powell and Sonja Larson to death; Larson had been raped before she died. The next day, Rolling raped and murdered Christa Hoyt in her duplex. Two days later, he pried open a sliding glass door and entered an apartment shared by Tracy Paules and Manny Tabboada. He wasn't expecting to find a large man sleeping there—Manny was a well-built two-hundred-pound guy—so he took him out first. Then he moved to Tracy's bedroom where he raped and murdered her. Because Rolling had mutilated his victims and staged the bodies for maximum shock value, the local press dubbed him The Gainesville Ripper.

Weapons in the House

"Many feel that firearms are the way to protect themselves. We disagree," says Lieutenant Paul Satkowski. "Guns in the home are twenty-two times more likely to be used for something other than self-defense." Police also believe there's a high risk—especially if you haven't had the training to handle a gun properly—that a home invader will turn the gun against you.

Here are some safer alternatives to a gun:

Place a kid-sized baseball bat under your bed, where it is close but not visible. (You don't want an intruder to use it on you.)

Keep a container of pepper spray or Mace in your bedside drawer.

Place your cell phone by your bed at night, with 911 on speed dial.

Install a deadbolt on your bedroom door.

Turn a closet into a panic room.

A Do-It-Yourself Panic Room

You can transform your closet into a panic room by installing a deadbolt lock on the inside of the door. Write a list of emergency contacts, such as your nearest neighbors' numbers, on the door. Rig up a working light, the kind that you can switch on and off. Put in a landline phone. Position a can of pepper spray or Mace so it is within easy reach.

What If You Hear an Intruder Break in?

If you hear a noise suggesting a stranger has gained entry, leave the premises through any accessible door or window—even a doggy door if you're tiny enough to fit through. If you have a roommate, don't run to warn her. It will only alert the invader to her presence, as well as your own. From outside you can knock quietly on your roommate's window and gesture for her to climb through the window. Leave the area immediately. Call 911 if you have your cell phone with you. Otherwise, ask a neighbor to make the call.

If you live with small children, decide in advance where you would all run if you heard an intruder breaking into the house: What escape route would you take? Where would you meet up? To make it less alarming, turn it into a game. Take inspiration from the Three Little Pigs folk tale, and practice fleeing the wolf.

What if you are unable to exit the premises?

1. Go to your panic room, lock yourself in, and call 911.
2. No panic room? Bolt your bedroom door with the deadlock, and call 911.

Should You Scream for Help?

If an intruder confronts you, should you scream for help? It depends on whether the neighbors would be able to hear you. If you're in an apartment building with thin walls, go ahead. But yell, "Fire! Call 911." The prospect of a fire spreading usually galvanizes neighbors into fast action, whereas they might not respond to the sound of a woman being terrorized. Sad but unfortunately true.

If you live in a house and there are no close neighbors, screaming might be a waste of time and energy. It could also backfire: the intruder might use excessive violence to shut you up. Try to keep a cool head, and look for an opportunity to use the "fight dirty" tactics or negotiation skills described in the next few chapters.

CHAPTER 15

The Warrior Woman

"If you can identify your attacker because he allows you to see his face or you know his name, it is all the more important to get away from him, even if he has a knife and you are risking injury. Because unless he's quite inexperienced, he's likely to kill you to leave no witnesses."
—ROGER DEPUE, THE FBI'S BEHAVIORAL SCIENCE UNIT.

Every soldier feels scared before a battle. Army training is designed to help soldiers overcome that fear. The goal is that no matter how disturbing the sights and sounds of combat, the sheer force of habit will turn the soldier into an effective fighter.

The war against women doesn't involve military-style weapons. Rape is the weapon. But victims also have a better chance of surviving it if they can quickly recall pre-planned strategies. In this chapter, we'll be discussing a range of options. But first, let's talk about when and if to acquiesce or fight back in a rape.

Acquiesce or Resist?

It was once believed that the safest course for a woman was to comply with her rapist. Law enforcement no longer gives that advice. Compliance isn't rewarded. The rapist expects her to comply. What he is not expecting is forceful resistance.

Resistance releases adrenalin, which helps the victim to think and act more clearly. Acquiescence does the opposite. It provokes the "freeze effect," where, due to extreme fear, the victim is unable to move. Someone experiencing that kind of paralysis isn't likely to recognize an opportunity to escape. And law enforcement believes she needs to be ready to seize any opportunity.

Behavioral profilers Daniel L. Carter, Robert A. Prentky, and Ann W. Burgess interviewed 389 rape survivors for the study, *Lessons learned for Response to Sexual Violence.* They concluded that when possible, escape should be the top priority, especially "if there are no weapons, if there are other people somewhere in the vicinity, and if there are no restraints because the probability of a successful flight will be increased."

The "Promise"

What if a predator promises to release you later if you follow orders? In such terrifying circumstances, it's normal to want to believe him. Police supervisor Sanford Strong explains: "Our intellect begins to analyze based on false assumptions: 'If I do as I'm told, he won't hurt me.' But predators don't keep their promises. David Gore recalls: "Of course I kept telling her constantly that if she did everything I asked and didn't cause any problems, I'd let her go later. She knew I was going to rape her but she thought that was all."

The thirty-six serial killers interviewed by the FBI for the *Sexual Homicide Study* made the same promise. It is just standard procedure, explained Dennis Rader: "You win if people think they are going to be okay, yeah they are going to be out of harm's way, you got them."

The predator's orders are in his best interests, not yours. Interpret them accordingly. For instance, "You're coming with me!" tells you he isn't able to do what he wants to you in the present location. "Don't scream, and you won't get hurt," indicates he is worried people will hear you scream, and come running. Since he's telling you what cards you hold, it's likely to be in your best interests to do the opposite of what he wants.

Animal prey fights back—slashing with their claws, biting and kicking, butting with their horns. Even if the chances of escape are slim to nil—he's bigger, he's faster, he's hungrier, and he has sharper teeth—they obey their survival instinct. Serial killer Danny Rolling urges victims to fight for their lives, too.

"Don't ever let an attacker get control. Fight for your life. Scream as loud as you can. Spray Mace in his face. Kick him in the balls. Scratch at his eyes."

The thirty-six serial killers in the FBI's *Sexual Homicide Study* told interviewers that a third of the time resistance by their victims led to increased violence. Even so, of their victims who didn't fight back, "all were murdered without exception." As Gary Ridgway (the Green River Killer) recalls: "I told them that if they stopped fighting I would let them go, but I was always going to kill them."

At the First Crime Scene

The riskiest time for a predator is at the first crime scene. If the woman screams, people might call 911. He might be tackled. Even if he escapes, there may be witnesses capable of identifying him in a lineup. He worries about unknown factors such as these with good reason. The first crime scene is your best opportunity to derail the abduction.

Writing about himself in the third person, Dennis Rader describes one failed abduction: "He walked up to his target, and grabbed her. But everything went wrong. The moment he lay his hands on her, she started screaming and punching at him. He couldn't control her arms. She'd gone insane on him. He didn't realize that a woman could be so strong. He ran like hell back toward his car. 'That was a big mistake,' he muttered to himself while heading back home."

In FBI jargon, what Rader encountered was "verbally confrontative resistance" combined with "physically confrontative resistance." In the FBI's *Lessons learned for Response to Sexual Violence*, the authors recommend verbally confrontative resistance as a woman's first line of defense. They suggest calling the attacker derogatory names, yelling "Leave me alone!" directly into his face, and screaming for help, so he'll get the message that there is no way you are going quietly. Serial killer Jerry Brudos recalls fleeing a situation of that kind: "She was screaming and she caught my finger in the trigger guard and damn near broke it. She was attracting attention, and I knew I had to get away from there. I managed to get loose of her."

Profiler Pat Brown recommends a scream "that tells the person who hears it what to do: 'Help! Help! Call the police!'" Candice DeLong suggests that "Fire! Call 911" will get a quicker response. Some profilers recommend, "He's got a bomb! Call 911." Some self-defense experts like a shout that draws people's attention to the predator's appearance: "Go away tall bearded man with the red shirt and Doc Martens." (The theory is that he'll feel exposed and at risk. It also embeds those details in your mind so you'll be able to retrieve them for police.)

Self-defense experts prefer shouting to screaming for the following two reasons:

a. Shouting originates from the diaphragm, and presents a more forceful stance than screaming, which comes from the throat.
b. Since a shout is projected upward from the diaphragm, it prepares a victim's body for taking a blow, rather than having the wind knocked out of her.

If the predator doesn't move, the woman should immediately follow up with physically confrontative resistance. "Attack the assaulter with moderate physical aggression. Hit, kick, punch, etcetera." Try to strike first. If your opponent makes the first move his blow may stun you too much for you to be able to fight.

"In no viable form of self-defense does a person wait for a predictable attack to occur before responding," observes security expert Gavin de Becker. "Not even the most spiritual martial arts master would tell students, 'First receive a substantial blow to the head so that you know your adversary means you ill. Then respond.'"

Fighting Moves

He's undeterred by verbal and physical confrontative resistance? He becomes more violent? Profiler Candice DeLong counsels: "A rapist who is abusive from the outset, physically and verbally, should be regarded as very dangerous." It's imperative that you escape this kind of UNSUB. This could be a fight for your life.

Stabilize your fighting stance by staying centered and low. Lean forward slightly so your weight is on the balls of your feet. A low center of gravity will keep your core tight and make it harder for the predator to control you.

Your goal is to resist being pushed to the ground, so you that can run when you get the chance. Place your strongest foot behind you and angle it slightly outward at thirty degrees. If he pushes you, your strong foot can maintain your balance.

Avoid unnecessary arm movements. Flailing your arms won't push the assailant away, and it wastes precious energy. The goal is to get your opponent off-balance. If he lunges at you, step back and swivel aside. Once he ends up sprawled on the ground, you will be able to make your escape. If he goes to grab your head with his arm, step back. If he grabs you in a tight hold, twist out of his grasp rather than pull.

If he is on top of you, prevent him from straddling your legs because it will limit your ability to escape. If you can't, you still have options. One of them is to wrap your legs around the attacker's waist very tightly. Use your quadriceps—the largest muscles located in your thighs—to squeeze the attacker's ribs, causing him to lose oxygen. Dig your heels into his legs and push him off. (An advantage for a girl wearing pants is that he won't be able to remove them in this position.)

Another move is to pull the attacker's head close to your chest, limiting his ability to use his hands. A head butt can also be effective, but it needs to be done right. Do not try to hit someone with your forehead against their forehead. Instead lean back slightly, and swing the side of your forehead into a small target area such as the nose, the temples, or the side of their jaw.

If he has grabbed you from behind, bend your knees and squat down, slumping forward. This position ensures a person—like a sack of potatoes—is difficult to throw. Now you have two powerful options:

1. Do a reverse head butt to break his nose or jaw.
2. Crush his toes. At the top of his feet is a network of tiny, fragile bones that can easily be broken if you drive your heel down hard on them. The attacker won't be expecting it, and since it is a very painful injury, he is likely to loosen his grip. This injury will make it very hard to chase you.

Case History: Jennifer Gilbert

As Jennifer Gilbert recalls, the day started out as "a sunny, gorgeous day." She was twenty-two years old, and she had traveled from Westchester to visit her old college roommate in New York City. Her friend had invited her to view her new apartment.

She remembers, "I was in her hallway ringing her doorbell when . . . bam bam bam." Jennifer had been followed from the subway. "I was alone, in the hall, with a man who was about to kill me. I remember yelling, 'Oh my God, he's stabbing me!'"

She harnessed her inner Warrior Woman. Though her attacker brutally stabbed her with a screwdriver thirty-seven times, Jennifer used all her strength to resist: "I fought, I kicked, I screamed, and somehow I got him off of me and I got to my feet. I have scars all over my body from the attack, faint little white lines all over, but I have no memory of feeling pain. What I felt was an instinctual, fierce, bottomless urge to fight."

What If He Has a Gun?

Is it safer to go quietly if he produces a weapon? Not necessarily. As police supervisor Sanford Strong explains, "Initial injury is far from the worst consequence of a violent crime." Authorities believe it's better to risk being knifed or shot than to be taken to a second crime scene.

Most serial killers strangle their victims; they only produce a gun to force compliance. Harvey Glatman told detectives he used the gun to "get her to a frame of mind where she would be docile." David Gore didn't consider using his police-issued gun to shoot his victim. "Shooting someone is impersonal," he explained.

The odds of survival usually improve if the victim takes off running. Serial rapists are rarely crack shots, but even a trained marksman finds it hard to hit a moving target. Gun experts say that the best chance of scoring a hit is one in twenty-five, and even then it would probably just result in a flesh wound. To make yourself even harder to hit, run zigzag, rather than in a straight line. If there are two victims, run in different directions. Even if the serial rapist manages to wound one, the other will have a chance to escape and contact the police.

Two Victims

Sometimes, two friends have been captured together. When an opportunity to escape arises, neither takes it because they are reluctant to abandon each other. While this shows admirable loyalty, it is counterproductive. The remaining victim has a better chance of being saved if her companion escapes. The preda-tor might let the second victim go in order to put as much distance as he can between him and the police.

CHAPTER 16

How To Fight Dirty

*"This requires the victim to convert fear into rage, and
a sense of helplessness into a battle for survival."*
— Forensic researchers Daniel L. Carter,
Robert A. Prentky, and Ann W. Burgess

n the FBI's *Sexual Homicide Study*, criminal profilers collected data on the 118 victims of thirty-six serial killers. Nine were still alive because they had managed to escape. The rest were murdered regardless of whether they attempted to escape or not. The profilers conclude, "Escape remains the best and safest of all measures. You should always be ready for escape."

Get ready to unleash your inner Warrior Woman. In this chapter you'll learn how to fight dirty. Do not hesitate. You may only get one chance. The eyes, ears, nose, throat, groin, and toes are the most vulnerable areas of the body. So that's where you can do serious injury. "The victim is not going to be arrested for kicking a rapist in the groin or gouging his eyes," attests security expert Gavin de Becker. "Bite, kick him in the testicles, gouge his eyes, break his nose, spray his face with Mace if that's what it takes to get free."

His Eyes

A person's eyes are extremely sensitive. Remember when you were a kid and you got sand in them? How they stung so much you couldn't see or move? Well, that's the crippling effect you're going for here. So if an assailant has his fingers around your throat, rather than trying to pry them off—a waste of your time and energy—follow FBI agent Candice DeLong's advice: "Go straight for his eyeballs with your fingers, jamming them into his head as hard as you can—don't be squeamish —and with no letup." The agony will paralyze the rapist. Not only won't he see you run off, he won't even know in which direction you were headed.

You can also gouge eyes by using thumbs instead of fingers. Grip the attacker's head, and push your thumb with full force into the eye socket. (If it's dark and you can't see properly, scan the face for his tear duct.) Drag your thumb in and across the eye. Meanwhile, so the rapist can't move away to free himself, pull the back of his head toward your thumb. The goal is to separate his eye from his head. With one of his eyes severely damaged, repeat with the other eye, or pummel him on that side of his head.

"Many people, women in particular, struggle with the idea of gouging eyes," acknowledges David Kahn, a popular Krav Maga instructor. "But when your life is in danger, you need to defend yourself."

His Ears

Grab the front of the attacker's head and slide your fingers behind his ear. It takes about seven pounds of pressure to tear an assailant's ear off. Grip the ear tightly and pull it toward your body with full force, at the same time pushing his head away from you.

If you're on the ground with him on top of you and your hands are pinned, you can bite the ear and try to pull it off that way.

His Throat

The throat is very sensitive. With sufficient force, you can kill an attacker by breaking his larynx. And if his jugular veins are constricted, your attacker could very well pass out.

To go for the throat, take a "knife hand" strike. To do this, curl your fingertips downward as if you were about to make a fist. Tuck your thumb next to your forefinger and tighten. This leaves your middle knuckles as the point where you will connect. Strike by leading the tips of your forefinger and middle finger straight into the throat of your assailant. Be forceful. Imagine you are aiming for a spot five inches in. Twist into your strike for more force and damage. You'll do twice the damage if you also pull the assailant's head into the attack.

His Nose

The nose is another fragile area that can be easily broken.

If you're upright, you can break an attacker's nose with a well-placed punch to the bridge of his nose. But you need to make the right fist and aim forcefully. Punch as if your real target is a point five inches past the nose, near the back of his head. The nose can also be effectively attacked with an elbow (if it's in close range of the nose) or a knee (if the attacker is bent over). To use your knee, lace your fingers behind his head and pull it closer, while you take a half step back. Then drive your knee into his nose.

The advantage to breaking his nose is that it will cause his eyes to water severely. It will also really hurt.

Making the Right Fist

Self-defense expert Lucas Wheeler recommends bringing your fingers together as if you were pushing a door open. "Curl the fingertips in and down at your knuckles so that your hand is only half closed," says Wheeler. "Then curl your fingers tightly into your palm, wrapping your thumb tightly across your first two digits. Your fist should feel like a rock, extremely powerful and rigid." When you strike, lead with your fore knuckle and middle knuckle. Keep your fist in line with your arm and your target. Maintain your balance before you strike at 100 percent power. Strike and commit. You may only have one chance.

The Groin

The most painful area to strike on a man's body is his groin.

If you're upright, grab the assailant and pull his body close, then knee him in the groin. Alternatively, if your knee is immobilized but your elbow is free, use it to shove him hard in the groin.

Another option might be even more effective. Stand gripping his testicles with one hand, pulling them out from his body and twisting them. With your other hand, shield your face and head from blows. Hold and twist his testicles until he's fallen to the ground, writhing in agony.

Once you have made your move, follow through. You must show him no mercy, because if he gains the upper hand, you will receive none.

CHAPTER 17

Hostage Negotiations

"The only alternative to not doing away with a person, it would seem to me, would be to release her. To let her go free. That seems to be the only alternative. And not a very fancy one for him under the circumstances."
— SERIAL KILLER TED BUNDY

Sometimes escape isn't possible. For example, the victim is bound, gagged and handcuffed, or there is no one else around for miles to hear her scream. If you can't escape, try to negotiate your way to freedom. In this chapter I'm going to tell you about verbal strategies that have proven successful in the past. You'll also read about strategies that experts say are best avoided.

The most futile strategy is *to attempt to reason*. "Too many victims have thought that they could reason a sex predator into letting them go without harming them," veteran profiler Candice DeLong remarks ruefully. Apart from being a waste of precious time, it's risky. The rapist is likely to increase his violence if he feels you're patronizing him.

Another tactic that seldom works is *to appeal to his better nature*. That's because he doesn't have one. As DeLong explains, "If the rapist/killer has demonstrated enough violence in his nature that he is attempting to kidnap a stranger, he is a psychopath." Since psychopaths lack empathy and conscience, there's little one can appeal to—except self-interest. And there you need to proceed carefully. The psychopath will react badly if he suspects you are trying to manipulate him.

The sexual psychopath is a frustrated individual. He is furious that other people aren't giving him the respect he "deserves." To reduce his anger, hostage negotiators recommend that you are polite and respectful. Once he calms down, engage him in conversation. Serial rapists are collectors of injustices. Many of them believe they have been disrespected and abused by women. Try to convey a sense of interest, concern or caring.

Also, the longer you can keep your captor talking, the better your chances of being released. Ted Bundy told homicide detective Robert Keppel he was unable to kill any girl he talked to for more than twenty minutes. Keppel comments: "Once the person had achieved some kind of foothold as a real person in Bundy's eyes, her reality was greater than his fantasy."

For the *Convicted Rapists Study*, criminal profilers interviewed 108 serial rapists and 389 of their victims to find out how the offenders had responded to different tactics by victims. We'll take a look at the most successful strategies first. Sometimes victims tried a variety of strategies before hitting on the one that worked.

Tactic: Humanizing Yourself

"Rape is a hostage situation," says police supervisor Sanford Strong. He tells his officers that "if they find themselves in hostage situations, not to let the gunman get them facedown on the ground. In that posture, it is too easy for him to depersonalize you—much easier than pulling the trigger when you're staring him in the eyes." Strong says the same thing applies to rape.

Try to humanize yourself. Introduce details from your life into the conversation. Serial killer Edmund Kemper let a victim go when—after spying a bottle of pills on the front seat of the car—the young woman commented that her father was on the same medication, then inquired in a caring manner about Kemper's health. After a brief conversation, he let her out of the car.

If you can make a human connection, you might be able to talk the predator into taking you to a more populated area. Profilers recommend something along the lines of "Let's go for a beer." From there, you're in a better position to make your escape.

Tactic: Disrupting the Fantasy

Veteran profiler Roy Hazelwood interviewed hundreds of serial rapists during his time with the BSU. He says they were all avid collectors of bondage and S&M pornography. They had been masturbating to fantasies involving sex and violence since their teens.

Rapists are obsessed with bringing their most exciting sexual fantasies to life. The problem is, as Edmund Kemper once complained, "Your life gets in the way." Because he doesn't want a victim's reality to spoil his fantasy, the predator tries to see her as an object. Jeffrey Dahmer describes his effort to detach: "I always try to not get to know the person too well. Made it seem like it was an inanimate object."

It's important to disrupt the predator's fantasy.

One woman recalls the moment when Ted Bundy freed her: "I said, 'My five-year-old's home alone, and she's going to wake up and she'll be alone.'" The woman didn't know Bundy was helping to raise his girlfriend's five-year-old daughter. It was a lucky coincidence. "He changed all of a sudden. Just like that. He drove onto a street with tall trees. He said, 'This is it—this is where you get out.'"

Tactic: "I'm not the person you're mad at."

If a victim asks, "What if I was someone you cared about? How would you feel about that?" she disrupts the unfolding of the fantasy. It's crucial, however, to keep the identity abstract. Experts warn against inserting an identity like "your wife" or "your girlfriend. " Often the victim is a stand-in for someone the rapist hates. (Usually an ex-wife or ex-girlfriend.) Keep it abstract so that the kidnapper can supply the identity of a person he cares about.

Another option is to remind him gently "I'm not the person you're mad at." Alternatively, you could try "How do you know that I'm a bitch? You've never met me before. I could be a nice person." Another approach that has worked in the past is "It sounds like you're really angry at someone, but it can't be me, because we've never even met before." Or, "I'm a total stranger. Why would you want to hurt me? I've never done anything to hurt you."

The profilers who conducted the *Convicted Rapists Study* found that the following strategies had not only been ineffective, they made things worse:

Tactic: Threatening With Repercussions

Don't warn the abductor that he will end up in jail. This threat reminds him that you have the power to send him there—if he lets you live. He will also see it as a challenge to his authority. A serial killer explained to Dr. Eric Hickey that he felt disrespected when his victim threatened him with jail. She had failed to understand that he was the boss: "I'm in control, I am playing the star role here."

Tactic: Offering Him a Deal

Offering the rapist a deal is another bad idea. Serial killer David Gore was outraged that a victim would try to negotiate. "Don't ask me why in the world she thought I'd do what *she* asked after I hunted her."

Tactic: Crying

Tears don't melt the ice-cold heart of a serial rapist. Worse, they tend to regard crying with contempt. Diane L. was one of only four victims to survive the I-5 killer. Randy Woodfield said the only reason he let Diane go was that while the rest of the women cried and begged to be released, Diane did not. She didn't seem to be afraid of him at all, and he respected her for it.

Tactic: Bringing Up the Women in His Life

"What if I was your mother/sister/wife?" is a question to avoid. Profilers warn that unless you know the predator's personal history, you can't anticipate the emotions it will trigger.

For instance, the question, "What if I was your sister?" would have enraged Edmund Kemper. He was insanely jealous of his sisters, believing his mother preferred them. The question, "What if I was your daughter?" could incense a predator involved in a child custody battle, by reminding him how much he hates the child's mother.

Tactic: Turning Him Off

Some victims had tried to turn the rapist off by claiming to have their period or to be experiencing stomach cramps. It didn't work because the rapist didn't care. A rapist is also unlikely to release a victim because she pleads that she is a virgin. In fact, he is more likely to be turned on by this information.

It's also a risky strategy to claim to have an STD. "I shiver when I hear women advised to forestall rape by claiming to have AIDS or a venereal disease," comments FBI profiler Candice DeLong. In the rapist's warped mind, they're "establishing themselves as 'whores,' deserving of punishment." As for trying to deter a rapist by "throwing up, urinating, defecating, or acting crazy," DeLong cautions that's risky as well: "Women have paid with their lives for disgusting rapists."

Tactic: Pretending to Enjoy the Sex

This strategy only frustrates the rapist. "I wouldn't try it," says DeLong, who has known cases where "getting sexual with a rapist, taking the initiative to arouse him or feigning enjoyment" has proven fatal.

Veteran profiler Robert Ressler defines rape the following way: " Rape is sexually deviant behavior that exhibits absolute disregard for the worth and value of an individual." What's implicit in this behavior is the victim's lack of consent. Believe it or not, most rapists are in relationships. They have consensual sex with a wife or girlfriend at home. Unfortunately, that's not what they're after.

So, when a victim appears to be enjoying the sex, she is upsetting the rapist's agenda, which is that she *not* enjoy the sex, because he has *forced it* upon her.

Final Word

It's my heartfelt wish that you are never in the kind of danger that requires you drawing upon the strategies in my book. And of course I acknowledge that if that happens, you might not get the chance to do so.

If you survived a rape, please walk away from a friend or family member insensitive enough to play Monday morning quarterback. "Unlike the person criticizing her choices," the veteran profiler John Douglas points out, "the rape victim doesn't have wisdom in hindsight. She must assess a horrifying and threatening situation at the moment it is happening."

There is only ever one goal: to escape with your life. And you accomplished that. "I have tremendous respect for any rape victim who lives through the ordeal," Douglas continues, "because as hard to believe as it may seem to some, if you're alive to tell about it, you have achieved a major victory."

To my mind, you deserve the kind of support we give to soldiers returning from war. You survived a terrifying experience. Well done. I'm glad you're here.

Epilogue

"Female alliances are the key to safety."
— GAVIN DE BECKER, SECURITY EXPERT

met Jessica when she was seventeen. There was a very pretty girl standing at my door wearing cut-off shorts and a halter-top. She had big brown eyes, a blonde ponytail, high cheekbones, and a captivating smile. However, it wasn't her beauty that I noticed first. It was Jessica's energy. When she walked in, the kitchen grew brighter.

For two summers, Jessica babysat my children. She was a delight to have around—eager to please, quick to laugh, and endlessly inventive. On rainy days, she would devise elaborate treasure hunts for my little boys, writing clues on bits of paper she scattered through the house. She was kind, playful and funny. In one of my favorite photos, she wields a plastic sword and shield. "En garde!" My sons loved her. I loved her. If I'd had a daughter, I would have wanted her to be like Jessica.

We said our good-byes the day before Jessica left for college. She had always dreamed of being an actress, and now she was about to enter a prestigious musical theater program. Jessica was excited, but also nervous. In one breath, she described feeling she was on the threshold of making her dreams come true, and in the next breath, she was wondering if she had enough talent to make it to Broadway. "You'll find out soon enough!" I joked. She laughed. "I'm sure I will!"

Six weeks later, Jessica's nude body was found in a field. According to police, she had been drugged, repeatedly raped, and savagely beaten for hours.

She was close to death. The perpetrator was never identified. Because of the brutality of the crime, police believed that it wasn't his first rape, nor was it likely to be his last.

Violence was not the end of Jessica's story, I'm happy to report. After spending a couple of months recovering from her horrific injuries, she left the hospital determined to make a new start. She changed her first name. She didn't return to college. She decided to move to another state, where nobody knew her.

Jessica went off the grid. She wanted to feel strong again. Independent. She joined a homesteading community. She lived by herself in a cabin in the woods. There was no electricity. She chopped her own firewood, shoveled snow and grew her own vegetables. Then one day another homesteader introduced her to a friend who was visiting from the nearest city. This man —a good person—eventually became her husband.

Today, Jessica has children of her own. She moved to the city to live with her husband. They live in a comfortable home, with a nice garden. Jessica seems content. But it saddens me that she never got to pursue her dream. Who knows whether she would have been a successful actress? The thing is she never got to find out. It wasn't a dream that Jessica surrendered; it was a dream that was taken away from her.

I will never forget the day I heard the dreadful news. For weeks after, I kept wondering if there was something I could have said to Jessica before she left, some advice that might have protected her. But, what? Despite the fact I was twenty years older, the only advice I could have given her was "Keep an eye on your drink."

Jessica wasn't drinking.

That's why I decided to start researching A Girl's Guide to the Criminal Mind. I wanted to find out what the experts—like criminal profilers, security experts, and sex crimes detectives— could tell women about how rapists think, and how to escape them. This is the book I wish I'd been able to give Jessica before she left for college.

It's been said that it takes a village to raise a child. The village has another responsibility as well: to protect that child. One way is to train her how to fight back effectively, which all animals teach their offspring; another way is to intervene when you see her in danger. She deserves both. Too often, she gets neither.

After the 9/11 attacks, the Department of Homeland Security's campaign "If you see something, say something," entered the collective unconsciousness. To this day, people quickly pull out their cell phones to call 911 if they see an unattended package or a suspicious vehicle. Yet when it comes to calling 911 about a rape, too many people avert their eyes and walk away from the victim instead. This behavior is so common that Candice DeLong—a former FBI lecturer on women's safety— always told her audiences: "If you are ever assaulted, never count on help."

Sometimes—as with the notorious Kitty Genovese case in New York City— rape ended in murder because witnesses did nothing. "The cases that upset me the most are the ones where lives could have been saved if the victim's fellow citizens bothered to intervene," FBI profiler Candice DeLong admits. "All it takes to be a hero is to pick up the phone."

There is no equivalent in the wild. Birds of a feather really do stick together. The black-capped chickadee not only alerts its companions when it spots a predator, it also informs them how big the predator is. Likewise, prey animals do not shrug off each other's safety. They inform other animals if a predator is nearby. Certain monkeys even developed warning calls that describe whether the threat is from a bird of prey above the trees, or from a ground predator below them.

In nature, prey animals have each other's backs—literally. They travel in a herd. They stay alert, and look out for each other. When a predator launches an attack, prey animals flee together, or they surround the predator, kicking, biting, or goring him with their antlers in their attempts to drive him away.

Gavin de Becker points out that when a female Bonobo is bullied by her mate, the other females will gather and chase him away. The famed security expert believes that women and girls should have each other's backs, too. "For too long the odds were stacked against the individual prey. It's time the herd took care of its own."

I'd welcome your thoughts on this subject. You can drop me a line at my website: alisonsummers.com, or find me on twitter @AlisonSummers8.

I hope you enjoyed *A Girl's Guide to the Criminal Mind*. It's part of an ongoing series. The next one *A Girl's Guide to Predators* will be available in late 2016.

Recommended Reading

Although my research for this book is complete, I continue to be impressed by the dedication of organizations advocating for victims of sexual violence, such as the Joyful Heart Foundation and GEMS. And I remain in awe of the criminal profilers, forensic psychiatrists, and psychologists who journey into dark minds to make the world safer for the rest of us.

Benson, Michael. *Murder in Connecticut.* The Lyons Press, 2008.

Black, Donald W., with C. Lindon Larson. *Bad Boys, Bad Men.* New York, NY: Oxford University Press, 1999.

Brady, Ian. *Gates of Janus.* Los Angeles: Feral House, 2001.

Brown, Pat with Bob Andelman. *The Profiler: My Life Hunting Serial Killers and Psychopaths.* Hyperion Books, 2010.

Brown, Pat. *Killing for Sport: Inside the Minds of Serial Killers.* New Millennium Press, 2003.

Brown, Pat. *How to Save your Daughter's Life: Straight Talk for Parents*. Health Communications Inc., 2012.

Burgess, Ann W., Allen G. Burgess, John E. Douglas, and Robert K. Ressler, eds. *Crime Classification Manual; A Standard System for Investigating and Classifying Violent Crimes*. Jossey-Bass Publishers, 1992.

Carter, Daniel, Robert A. Prentky, and Ann W. Burgess. "Victims: Lessons Learned for Responses to Sexual Violence," *Journal of Interpersonal Violence*, 1(1) 1986: 73–98.

Cleckley, Hervey. *The Mask of Sanity*. 5th Ed. Mosby, 1976.

De Becker, Gavin. *Protecting the Gift: Keeping Children and Teenagers Safe (and Parents Sane)*. New York, NY: Dell Publishing, 1999.

DeLong, Candice. *Special Agent: My Life on the Front Lines as a Woman in the FBI* Hyperion, 2001.

Depue, Roger L. with Susan Schindehette. *Between Good and Evil*. New York, NY: Grand Central Publishing, 2005.

Douglas, John E., and Mark Olshaker. *Obsession*. New York, NY: Scribner, 1998.

Douglas, John E., and Mark Olshaker. *The Cases that Haunt Us*. Pocket Star Books, 2001.

Douglas, John E., and Mark Olshaker. *Mindhunter: Inside the FBI's Elite Serial Crime Unit*. Pocket Star Books, 1995.

Furio, Jennifer, *The Serial Killer Letters*. The Charles Press, 1998.

Hare, Robert D. *Without Conscience*. New York, NY: The Guilford Press, 1999.

Hazelwood, Roy, and Stephen Michaud. *Dark Dreams: Sexual Violence, Homicide and the Criminal Mind*. St. Martin's Press, 2001.

Hickey, Eric W. *Serial Murderers and Their Victims*. Stamford, CT: Wadsworth Thomas Learning, 2002.

Kendall, Elizabeth. *The Phantom Prince*. Seattle: Madrona Publishers, 1981.

Keppel, Robert D. *Signature Killers*. New York, NY: Pocket Books, 1997.

Keppel, Robert D., with William J. Birnes. *The Riverman*. New York, NY: Pocket Books, 2005.

Levin, Jack. *Serial Killers and Sadistic Murderers*. Amherst, NY: Prometheus Books, 2008.

Magid, Ken, and Carole A. McKelvey. *High Risk: Children without a Conscience*. Golden, Colorado: Bantam; M & M Publishing, 1987.

McCrary, Gregg O. *The Unknown Darkness*. New York, NY: Harper Collins, 2003.

Meloy, Dr. J. Reid. *The Psychopathic Mind: Origins, Dynamics, and Treatment*. Lanham, Maryland: Rowman & Littlefield Publishers, Inc., 1998.

Meloy, Dr. J Reid. *Violent Attachments*. Jason Aronson Inc., 1992.

Michaud, Stephen G., and Hugh Aynesworth. *Ted Bundy: Conversations With A Killer (The Death Row Interviews)*. Irving, Texas: Authorlink Press, 2000.

Millon, Theodore, Erik Simonsen, Morton Birket-Smith, and Roger D. Davis, eds. *Psychopathy*. New York, NY: The Guilford Press, 1998.

Morrison, Dr. Helen, and Harold Goldberg. *My Life among the Serial Killers*. New York, NY: Avon Books, 2004.

Nelson, Polly. *Defending the Devil*. New York, NY: William Morrow and Company, Inc., 1994.

Ramsland, Katherine. *The Human Predator.* Berkeley Books, 2005.

Ramsland, Katherine. *The Criminal Mind: A Writer's Guide to Forensic Psychology.* Writer's Digest Books, 2002.

Reichert, Sheriff David. *Chasing the Devil: My Twenty-Year Quest to Capture the Green River Killer.* Little Brown and Company, 2004.

Ressler, Robert K., and Tom Shachtman. *I Have Lived in the Monster.* New York, NY: St. Martin's Press, 1997.

Ressler, Robert K., Ann W. Burgess, and John E. Douglas. *Sexual Homicide: Patterns and Motives.* New York: The Free Press, 1996.

Restak, Richard. *The Self Seekers.* Garden City, New York: Doubleday Company, Inc., 1982.

Rule, Anne. *The Stranger Beside Me.* New York, NY: W.W. Norton & Company, Inc.

Samenow, Stanton E. *Inside the Criminal Mind.* New York, NY: Crown Publishers, 1984.

Sands, Stella. *The Dating Game Killer.* St. Martin's Paperbacks, 2011.

Schober, Jeff with Det. Dennis Delano. *The Bike Path Rapist.* The Lyons Press, 2009.

Snortland, Ellen. *Beauty Bites Beast: Awakening the Warrior within Women and Girls.* B3Books, 1998.

Stone, Dr. Michael H. *The Anatomy of Evil.* Amherst, New York: Prometheus Books, 2009.

Stout, Dr. Martha. *The Sociopath Next Door.* New York: Broadway Books, 2005.

Strand, Ginger. *Killer on the Road: Violence and the American Interstate*. Austin: University of Texas Press, 2012.

Jane Velez-Mitchell. *Secrets Can Be Murder: The Killer Next Door*. Touchstone, 2007.

Yochelson, Dr. Samuel, and Dr. Stanton E. Samenow. *The Criminal Personality*. Vol. 1. Lanham, Maryland: Rowman & Littlefield Publishers, Inc., 1976.

Acknowledgements

The author gratefully acknowledges the valuable suggestions, encouragement and support of Lindsey Alexander, Linda Anthony, Selwa Anthony, Sam Carey, Doris Downes, Jesse Gordon, Herb Hernandez, Nina Keneally, Susan Bliss Purdy, Aviva Slesin, Charley Summers and Lucas Wheeler.

About the Author

Alison Summers lives in Brooklyn. Her first book, *The Girl's Guide to Predators*, was published by Pan Macmillan in Australia and New Zealand. It will be available soon in the United States and Canada. She also co-wrote (with Deb Filler) and directed an award-winning play, *Punch Me in the Stomach*, which was produced by New York Theater Workshop, and toured North America, Europe, Australia, and New Zealand.

Readers can connect with the author online at:
Twitter: @AlisonSummers8
Facebook: https://m.facebook.com/profile.php?id=375946552534356
Website: www.alisonsummers.com

Made in the USA
Lexington, KY
14 September 2019